KATHMANDU: THE FORBIDDEN VALLEY

Library of Congress
Cataloging-in-Publication Data
Lloyd, R. Ian
    Kathmandu: The Forbidden Valley /
      R. Ian Lloyd & Wendy Moore.
     p. cm.
   ISBN 0-312-04610-3: $40.00
  1. Kathmandu Valley (Nepal)—
Description and travel.
  2. Kathmandu Valley (Nepal)—
Description and travel-views.
  I. Moore, Wendy.
  II. Title.
  DS495.8.K3L56   1990   90-933454
  954.96-dc20   CIP

ISBN 0-312-046103

First published in Singapore by R. Ian Lloyd
Productions Pte Ltd.

First U.S. Edition
10 9 8 7 6 5 4 3 2 1

KATHMANDU
THE FORBIDDEN VALLEY

KATHMANDU
THE FORBIDDEN VALLEY

Photography by R. Ian Lloyd • Written by Wendy Moore
Designed by Genevieve Gigi Schiemann • Edited by Joseph R. Yogerst

St. Martin's Press
New York

CONTENTS

THE KATHMANDU VALLEY

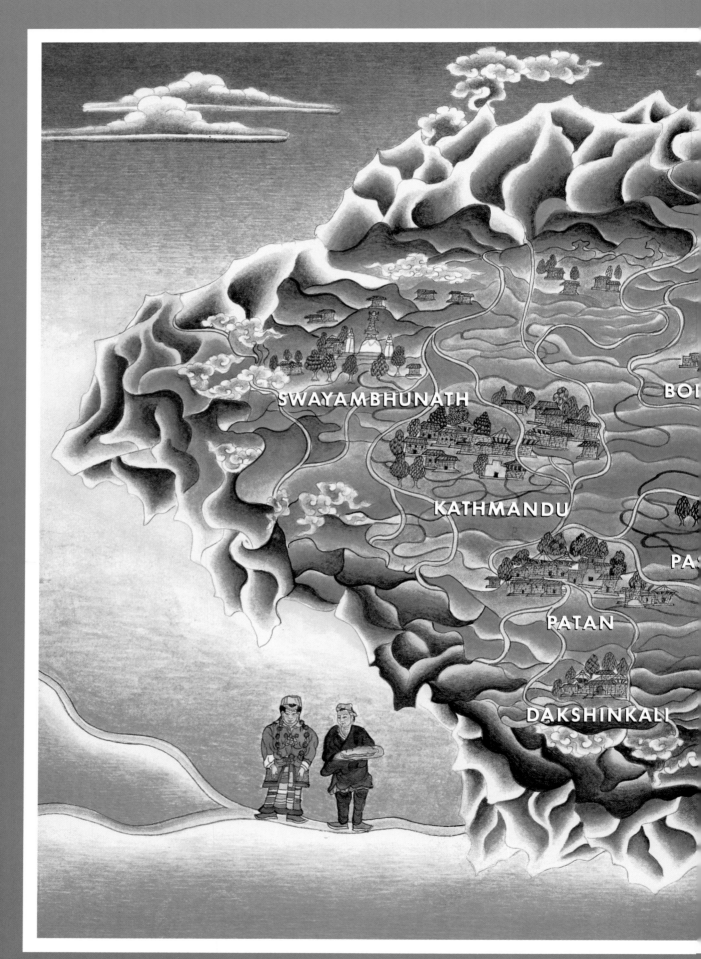

CHANGU NARAYAN

NATH

BHAKTAPUR

PATINATH

UNGAMATI

The Medieval Kingdom

Bathed in mellow, early morning light, a village woman makes her way to market along the tree-lined road to Bhaktapur, one of the three medieval kingdoms of the valley, fourteen kilometres east of Kathmandu.

I know a place, hidden like a "paradise lost" amongst the lofty Himalayas, where you can almost forget the 20th century exists. A strange and fascinating place where cities and towns appear like scenes from a medieval pageant. A Brueghel canvas, yet infinitely more exotic. For here, amid the golden-roofed pagodas and multi-storied palaces, dwell virgin goddesses and a living God-King. Kathmandu reminds me of those mysterious, romantic, inaccessible valleys found in romance novels.

It had been nearly twenty years since I last ventured along the overland route into the valley. It was a gruelling trip then, and remains so today. But to truly appreciate the vale's incredible isolation and its privileged oasis situation among the chaos of its mountainous world, one must journey along the original road, the ancient trade route.

Forty years ago this highway was a mere track and the journey into the forbidden valley was only for the chosen few. Foreigners were barred from entering this feudal kingdom until the middle of this century. Kathmandu attained a reputation as being "more secret than Mecca." Even the intrepid Marco Polo, who visited almost everywhere in Asia in the 13th century, commented that "the country is wild and mountainous and is little frequented by strangers, whose visits the king discourages." Naturally, these barriers to investigation only helped to strengthen the growing attraction and mystique of this Himalayan kingdom.

Sylvain Levi, a French orientalist, managed to wangle his way into Nepal for a two-month sojourn in the spring of 1898. Inaccessibility had its price, as Levi discovered to his chagrin. He complained that the journey from Calcutta to Nepal was "rather ruinous" — for the same price (400 rupees

or 650 francs) he had travelled from Marseilles to Bombay in far greater comfort than the palanquin which bore him into the Kathmandu Valley. In this "dandy chair" were all his bedding, provisions and household goods. He marvelled at the bearers' strength and speed, finding it impossible to walk with them. "One must run or jump into the palanquin," writes Levi. "One feels by degrees, and very soon, hurt all over."

Even in the early 1950s, mountaineer Tom Weir and his Scottish Nepal Expedition had to walk across the two mountain ranges that barred access to the Vale of Kathmandu. He described the track, "as an uncompromising green slope cleft by gullies, up which we could see a wavering

Left: Only from the air is it evident that Bodhnath stupa, Nepal's largest Buddhist relic-mound, is designed as a *mandala*, a sacred religious diagram composed of concentric circles within squares. Above: Straddling a dragon-back ridge twelve kilometres east of Kathmandu is Changu Narayan, the oldest Vishnu temple in Nepal and a repository of priceless stone sculpture, including the oldest inscription found in the valley.

path dotted with the bent backs of coolies." Along this Asiatic highway moved herds of goats and buffaloes, hordes of porters hauling goods, parties of Gurkha soldiers on leave from service to the British Raj and wealthy Nepalese nobles reclining on litters. Weir felt, like many travellers even today, that "we had stepped into the 17th century."

Once in Kathmandu these early tourists found that all of the fifty or so cars that plied the city's streets had literally been manhandled over that same awesome mountain track. Fully-assembled, the vehicles had been bound to bamboo pallets and shouldered over the ranges by dozens of struggling, heaving porters.

And now, here it is almost two decades later, as I wait with anticipation for the moment when I will mount the crest of that last obstructing mountain range and catch my first glimpse of the enchanted vale which has moved so many writers to superlatives. It was the "valle bellissima" of the 17th-century Capuchin missionaries, while 19th-century explorer

Kurt Boeck described it as a "picture of fairytale beauty, such as is not to be found anywhere else in the world."

   I am not disappointed. The view is just as amazing as I, and all the travellers before me, have waxed lyrical about. We top the rim of a giant bowl to see a green fertile valley spread out below. Although it measures a mere 24 kilometres long by 19 kilometres wide, the valley is an exceptional place; due to its size and wealth, a novelty in this part of the world. Kathmandu, a red-roofed city, sprawls across the valley floor where the silvery serpentine Bagmati, Nepal's holiest stream, finds its way. Gleaming pagodas rear from the heart of the old city and punctuate the skyline of lesser towns perched on ridges and nestled among the terraces of this intensely culti-

Left: On the road to Changu Narayan, in the eastern Kathmandu Valley, mud-brick houses with thatched roofs cluster on the tops of ridges. Encircling terraced fields hug the contour lines of the hills and ascend the slopes like giant stairways, cleverly irrigated by ancient water systems tapped from mountain streams.

Right: During the October harvest season, women of the traditional Newar farming caste, known as Jyapu, work as hard as their menfolk. Head-bands support cumbersome loads of ricestalks which they carry to their homes as winter fodder for livestock.

vated vale. And all about are the folds of the great encircling hills, some over 3,000 metres high, mountains in any other part of the world. Clouds from a late monsoon still linger, but then the sun came blazing out from an afternoon of gloom, radiating on dull brick and lighting it up like burnished copper. A hilltop shrine glitters like gold and the far hillsides are illuminated in sharp relief, every valley and ridge shadowed like the folds in a velvet cloak. Then in the east, the flash of a rainbow crowns a peak, an electric prism of colour spearing a high ridge and showering light on golden fields that have already been harvested. But across the northern horizon, the mighty Himalayas lay hidden under spectacular wads of cumulus which seem to stretch across the whole Tibetan skyline. I yearn for them to break formation. Just once, for an instant, the clouds split and shooting up to an impossible height is a great massif, apparently hanging in the

Lofty Himalayan peaks, almost 8,000 metres high, soar above the ridge at Nagarkot, 35 kilometres from Kathmandu on the eastern rim of the valley. During winter, October through March, the lodges which hug the 2,000 metre-high ridge offer one of the greatest mountain vistas in the world, a 300-kilometre panorama from the Annapurna range in the west to Mount Everest in the east. Early birds who brave freezing pre-dawn temperatures are rewarded with a spectacular sunrise over Everest, also known by its Nepalese name of Sagarmatha, the highest point on earth.

sky, its narrow corniced ridges glistening in the late afternoon sun. Then it's gone, like a tease. But I know that behind that mass of vapourous cloud are the most magnificent mountains on earth, the awe-inspiring backdrop to Kathmandu and the Abode of the Gods, benevolent and malevolent, who have always played a major role in the valley's life.

This backdrop lay under a shroud of cloud for a week and then one evening it rained, a good steady rhythm all night, and when I awake the sky is a clear porcelain blue. Rubbing the sleep from my eyes, I stumble to the rooftop and am rewarded with a sight of the triangular snow-capped Ganesh Himal, the dwelling place of the elephant-headed god, Ganesh, a favourite of the Nepalese for he brings

success to all undertakings. His abode soars above the valley, an ethereal white, so pure and pristine. Despite the distance, perhaps sixty kilometres as the crow flies, the knife-like ridges and the snow fields appear near. It's quite logical that they have from time immemorial been associated with the gods, for what mortal man could live in such inhospitable realms. The idea of humans with ice axes and spiked crampons tramping across those ridiculously snowy heights is as incredible and unconnected to life on earth as men in space suits leaping around on a TV moon. As I gaze across the warm sunny fields of ripening paddy, where villagers are happily harvesting their crops, the valley seems so warm and comfortable, compared to those icy forbidden realms.

Perhaps the gods had this feeling, for back in the mists of time it appears they also liked to venture into the valley. According to ancient chronicles and verified by modern geologists, the Kathmandu Valley was once a lake. Known as Nag-hrad, the lake was the abode of a pantheon of serpent dieties, the Nagas. They are still worshipped today and even have their own festival, Naga Panchami, the Day of the Snake Gods. On this day, paper images of writhing reptiles are pasted over doorways and offerings are made to appease the powerful Nagas, for when properly assuaged they bring vital rains and guard the family wealth.

Surrounded by forested hills full of flowers and

Left: Kathmandu has always been a great market town, drawing merchants from the neighbouring valleys and even luring salesmen, like this banana vendor, all the way over the passes from the Indian Terai. This itinerant merchant is from Bihar, the poorest state in India, which shares a common border with Nepal.

Right: Two Nepalese workers take a break in the sun on the lower steps of the Shiva-Parvati Temple House in Kathmandu's Durbar Square.

A woollen shawl wrapped about her head and shoulders to keep out the winter chill, her skin coloured nut-brown from years of labouring under the high-altitude sun, this Nepalese farm woman leaves the portico of her neighbourhood temple. Her morning blessings to the gods completed, she will now prepare for another day's work in the fields, as her ancestors have done for centuries.

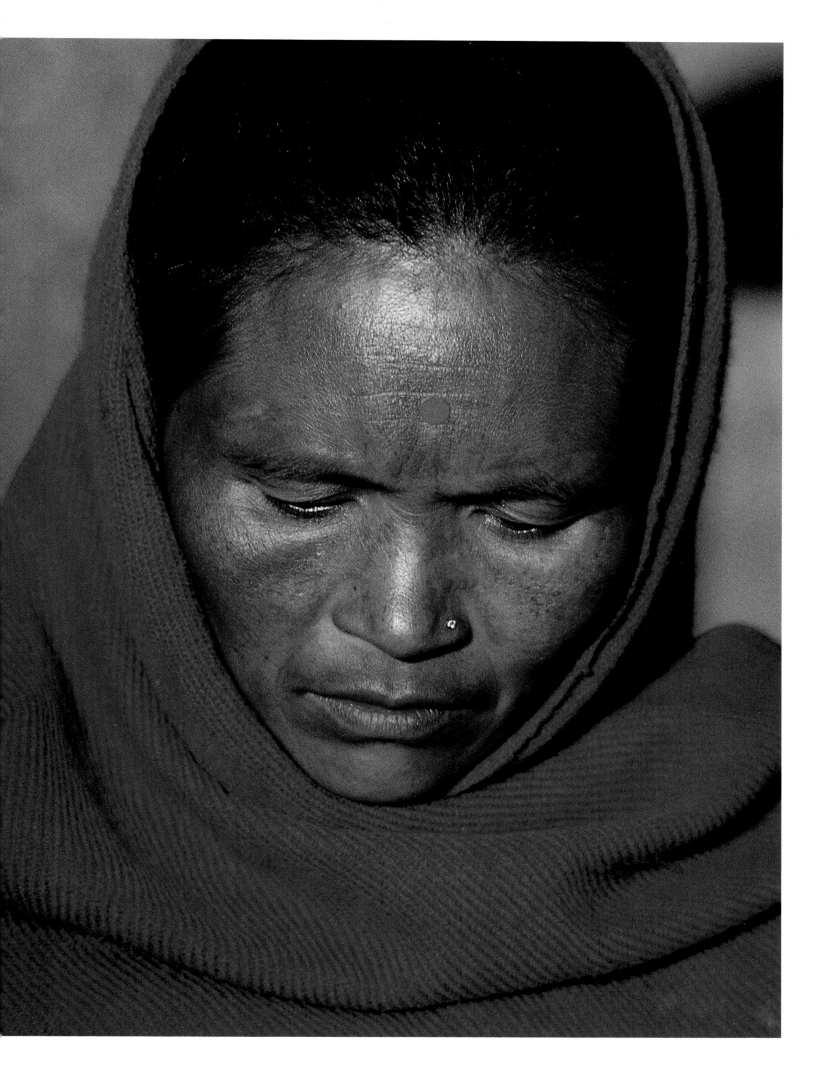

fragrant herbs, the idyllic lake attracted sages and seers who came to meditate in the lakeside caves. One day, a fabulous lotus in full flower appeared on the lake's surface. Emanating from the bloom was a radiant blue flame. Ancient scriptures say this was none other than Adi Buddha, the Self-Existent One known as Swayambhu. This sacred act took place near a hill now called Swayambhunath, subsequently covered with monasteries, temples and a famed stupa with "all-seeing eyes" which overlook Kathmandu. Epochs later, Manjushree, a divine saint from China, who had made a pilgrimage to the sacred lake to worship the holy flame, decided to drain the water and make the valley habitable for mankind. With one blow of his mighty sword he parted the hills and water gushed

out of the valley through the narrow ravine known today as Chobar Gorge. Manjushree's followers and disciples colonized and cultivated the vale, built temples and monasteries and founded a city known as Manjupatan which spread between Pashupatinath and Swayambhunath. Brahma, Vishnu and Shiva, the great Hindu gods, came down to visit from their lofty Himalayan dwellings and, at the sites of these legendary outings, temples sprung up across the enchanted vale.

These shrines multiplied until they outnumbered the houses, a fact that seems relevant even today. When Percival Landon, the historian, visited the valley in 1928, he was surprised to see that most of the temples were being utilized. This "cannot fail to strike even the most casual observer...that there are few ruins in the Valley. The great temples in India often lay deserted, mere goals of the antiquarian and the tourist, here [in the Kathmandu Valley] they are living and venerated..."

Left: Heavy wooden doors covered with embossed metal are characteristic of palace entrances built by the 17th-century Malla rulers. This bronzework was done in the repousse method, sheet metal hammered into shape from the reverse side, a technique used by Newar craftsmen since the 12th century.

Right: Shiva Ram Rana Magar, a guard at the Hanuman Dhoka palace in Kathmandu, is assisted at the guardhouse by Chinyaman Dhoke, an old royal retainer.

As Hindus traditionally believe that the greatness and salvation of a woman depends upon her devotion to her husband, female education has obviously been of low priority in the past. Recently conditions have improved and this young student, proudly wearing her school tunic, is the first girl in her family to receive formal education. Female literacy, however, is still a mere five percent in urban areas and practically non-existent in the villages.

CHAPTER 2

Ancient Trade Routes

There is a narrow roadway, a most ancient route, which carves its way diagonally through the heart of old Kathmandu. Here, where the old townhouses almost meet overhead, sheltering a maze of open-fronted shops and markets, is the city's commercial hub which once stood at the crossroads of the great trade routes, connecting Nepal to India and reaching over the mountains into Tibet and China.

For centuries, Nepalese porters have paced these ancient trails, backpacking loads of salt, wool and grain through the high mountain passes and over the hilly route to India, returning with spices, cloth and rice. These are no mere paths, but wide and often paved routes which form a seemingly infinite stone staircase rising over mighty slopes and cutting into the sides of great gorges.

Early in the morning, long before dawn, the trails that lead down to this hub are alive with porters bringing baskets of firewood, vegetables, grains and terracotta wares to the ancient bazaars of Asan Tole and Indra Chowk, where Newar merchants still carry on traditional trades that began over 2,000 years ago. For Kathmandu was, and still is, the greatest market town of the Himalayas.

The world is familiar with the *khukri* wielding Gurkhas and the mountaineering Sherpas. But the Newars — the valley's original people and the creators of Nepalese culture — are still little known outside the region. Newars made the valley what it is today: their cultivators tilled and terraced the fields; their architects and craftsmen built and adorned the pagodas; and their age-old traditions, rituals and festivals have remained intact and unique over the centuries, even after succumbing to the rule of the Goth-like Gurkhas in the 18th century.

Like glow-worms swarming through the night, shoppers in Kathmandu's Asan Tole weave their way through the narrow bazaar. This has been the traditional trading hub of the old city since medieval times, a crossroads of ancient trade routes which linked Nepal with the markets of India and China.

Above: Wiry Tamang porters, carrying their *doko* baskets by headstraps, trudge through Kathmandu's Basantapur Square in the late afternoon. The Tamang follow a form of Tibetan Buddhism and live on the rim of the Kathmandu Valley and well beyond it. Many are farmers who scrape a living from plots perched high on the surrounding hillsides. The only way to get their produce to market is to backpack it down the steep trails which wind to the cities and towns on the valley floor. Right: Traditional three-storey shop houses with overhanging balconies flank the narrow road to Indra Chowk, the crowded wool bazaar in the heart of old Kathmandu.

From where the Newars came, and when, has long been a disputed question in Nepalese history. Various theories abound. Some historians say they arrived with a dynasty of cowherder kings from the plains of the subcontinent, while others maintain they descended from ancient south Indian tribes or a Mongolian strain. The Newars believe they were the original valley dwellers who arrived with Manjushree, the drainer of the lake that was formerly Kathmandu, and no amount of investigation has ever proved otherwise. In fact, the Newari language has more in common with the Tibeto-Burman languages of the Himalayas than with Nepali, the lingua franca of Nepal which derives from northern Indian dialects and was the tongue of the Gurkhas, who claim their descent from the Rajputs. Even the name Nepal, some scholars maintain, is a deformation of "Newar," for up until recent times the term was never used by the hill people outside the valley to describe anything other than Kathmandu and its surrounding vale.

In the core of the old city, along a narrow street, beside a temple where children play on the backs of guardian stone lions, is a cupboard-sized workshop tucked under a wooden frieze carved with griffins and garudas. Inside, sitting cross-legged and dressed in beige-coloured pipe-stem trousers, long overshirt and nifty waistcoat topped with a brimless hat, an old Newar goldsmith patiently crafts an exquisite gold pendant. Under the light of a naked bulb he picks up a drop of solder with the moistened tip of a feather, applies it to the ornament and then heats it by blowing through a copper pipe onto coals in a terracotta bowl. Apart from the electric light, his methods and tools are little changed from ancient times. For Kathmandu, even today, is

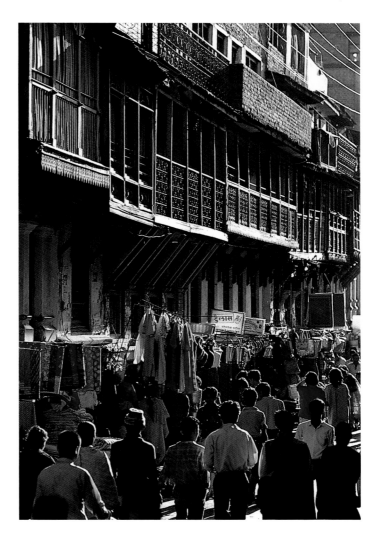

Firewood sellers await customers on the steps of a pagoda in Kathmandu's Durbar Square. Not so long ago forests covered the surrounding hills, but with population pressures and more land being cleared for farming, the trees have been largely depleted for fuel. Reforestation has little hope of success as long as there is no cheap alternative to wood.

a hive of goldsmiths, brassworkers and woodcarvers, carrying on the medieval trades of their revered ancestors whose sculptured ornaments and religious idols were sought after by rulers and patrons throughout the eastern world. It is said their renown even reached Kublai Khan who asked for Nepali artisans to build a golden temple in Tibet. Arniko, a famed architect, bronze-caster and painter, journeyed to Lhasa with his band of craftsmen, built and decorated the great golden stupa of the Sa-Sakya monastery and then proceeded to China at the invitation of the great khan himself. Arniko is credited with introducing bronze casting to Tibet. But he wasn't the first Newar to impress the Tibetans for, as legends go, Buddhism was actually introduced to the Tibetan court by a Newar princess in the 7th century. Bhrikuti, sent in marriage to King Tsrong-tsong Gompo, was the daughter of the mighty Nepalese King Amsuvarman whose golden palace, a Chinese chronicler reports, was seven storeys high and encrusted with gems and pearls. As part of her dowry, she brought Lord Buddha's bronze begging bowl and she so impressed the Tibetans with her faith and piety that she was immortalised as an incarnation of the Harita Tara, or Green Tara.

After Tibet's acceptance of Buddhism, trade flourished between the two kingdoms, as Newar craftsmen were needed to produce bronze idols for the newly-converted land. Artisans and merchants made the long, cold trek over the mountain passes to Lhasa where they established a permanent Newar colony. Daniel Wright, the historian, relates that even as late as 1877 there were some 3,000 Nepalese in Lhasa who had their own consul, or resident, known as a *vakil*. Many of these travelling merchants were revered by their fellow countrymen as men of valour and integrity, for they brought salt and other necessities of life back to the secluded Kathmandu Valley. Not only did they have to brave the chilly Tibetan Plateau, its perilous gorges and treacherous passes, but the trip to India through the malaria infested jungles was considered an equally awesome feat. Often the merchants were greeted on their return with rousing celebrations, shouldered through the streets on garlanded palanquins. One famous trader, Singha Saratha Bahu, was deified and is still feted every year on his festival day, the Chakandeo Jatra. He took 100 assistants to Lhasa where they fell under the spell of beautiful Tibetan women who were actually demons in disguise. Singha was the only one to escape the bewitching females. He flew home on a giant white steed, arriving in Kathmandu on the full-moon day of the Holi celebration. Since then, on this day, an image of Singha is carried through the streets of the old city.

Yet the deity closest to mercantile hearts — found in villages and towns wherever Newar traders have set up

Gleaming copper and brassware engulf a Newar vendor in the jam-packed Khel Tole, the oldest section of the diagonal trade route which slices across downtown Kathmandu. Bulbous, copper water urns are preferred by most valley women, as they are light, portable and a perfect shape to rest on the women's cummerbunds, with the neck of the urn crooked under their arm. The metal keeps the water cool even on hot summer days. Housewives keep their metalwares clean and shiny by rubbing them with ashes.

At festival times, stalls are set up in busy bazaars specializing in ready-made offerings for the innumerable *pujas*, or worship ceremonies. This girl sells wood-block prints with images of the gods, used to adorn the shrines and even car grilles after the blood sacrifices of the Dasain festival.

Business is so brisk along the old trade route near Indra Chowk that vendors even set up shop on the steps of store fronts. This Newari woman sits surrounded by bags of dried grains, beans and peas – the basics of Nepalese cuisine. The local favourite is *dhal*, a lentil which is boiled into a thick broth and eaten with rice and curries. Known as *dhal bhaat*, this is the traditional Nepali meal. For most Nepalese, meat is a luxury only served on festive occasions and lentils act as a substitute, providing much needed protein.

business — is the Samson-like Bhimsen, an incarnation of Shiva and the guardian deity of all merchants and tradesmen. On the banks of the Vishnumati River, where the old trade route leaves the city to continue over the hills to India, is a temple dedicated to Bhimsen. At the annual Bhimsen Puja, after the merchants have completed a 24-hour fast in his honour, a fierce scarlet-faced, moustachioed image of the god is drenched in the sacrificial blood of dozens of buffaloes, goats and chickens, to ensure prosperous trading for the year ahead. Not so long ago, before the Chinese communists took over Tibet, a Newar was chosen every twelve years to represent Bhimsen and journey to Lhasa in order to bless the Newar merchants in residence there.

I took a stroll along the old trade route, where business is as brisk today as it has been for centuries, to Asan Tole, the heart of the grain market and centre for just about every other commodity. Traffic slows to a crawl and over the clanging of temple chimes, the ringing of bicycle bells, the beeping of motorbikes and the occasional honking of car horns, the air is alive with the cry of hawkers. Here, at the five-way intersection that is Asan Tole, the road *is* the market and the aura of the great medieval trade routes lingers.

Under the carved and decorated facades of antique brick townhouses are dozens of shops, overflowing with various sights, smells and colours. A pungent aroma drifts from a sunny corner where only inches away from the traffic, three men are dealing in turmeric, their hands and forearms stained a spicy yellow. A wall of long white radishes is piled against a metal grille which supports a rack of votive lamps at the shrine of Annapurna Mai, the grain goddess and guard-

ian deity of Asan Tole. Dozens of fruit and vegetable vendors shelter under a sea of umbrellas where produce from the fertile valley and its terraced fields is artfully displayed in wickerwork baskets. There are pale pink radishes, creamy cauliflowers, green and white spring onions, autumnal-toned tomatoes, bunches of feathery herbs, small round potatoes from the Sherpa highlands, shining indigo eggplants and, everywhere, pale yellow guavas, for their season is now in full swing. Weaving his way through the centre of the bustling square, a porter shoulders a delicate load of fresh yoghurt in terracotta bowls hanging from his bamboo shoulder pole. A khaki-clad policeman half-heartedly attempts to move along a group of banana sellers, travelling salesmen from the plains

of Bihar who are attempting to under-sell the local fruit prices. But as soon as the constable wanders on, the tenacious traders sneak back into position – for where else is trade as brisk as in Asan Tole? A young Brahmin strolls from shop to shop, his brass tray piled high with marigold flowers and sacred vermilion powder. A vendor presses a *tikka* powder on his forehead, places a few golden petals on his hair-parting and drops a 25 paisa coin on the tray. The boy moves on to the next supplicant, who is eager to please the gods and so gain favour in the day's trading.

I follow a porter down the old trade route to Khel Tole. He's carrying a three-seater lounge chair on his back and bounding along like it's a sack of feathers. A sacred cow raises its tail and deposits a steaming dung cake right at my feet. Stretched across an old carved shopfront is a white cloth banner proclaiming in rather odd English, "Let's dwell our city by keeping it clean — Balkumari Youth Association." This is an uphill task in a city where buildings, roads and even the sanitation system are still medieval. Late last century, the British Resident's surgeon wrote that he thought it impossible to clean the drains without knocking down the entire city. His drastic approach fell on deaf ears.

At Khel Tole, Tibetan rugs drape from upstairs windows and painted puppets dangle from shops specialising in *thangka* paintings for tourists, but there is no mistaking the fact that this trading centre still relies on local business. Cloth merchants in stockinged feet lounge in their shops, surrounded by bolts of colourful fabrics. There are opulent saris with gold hems for the rich townswomen, lustrous red velvet for the blouses of hilltribe women and rolls of the traditional black-and-red blockprinted cotton used for quilts and shawls. Squatting at one of the fabric shops is a group of Magar ladies, sporting prominent gold nose rings, their long oiled braids

Butchery is considered a low-caste occupation among Hindus, and butcher shops are always situated in the part of town designated to that caste. Delivery men still trundle trishaws full of bloody carcasses through the city's

streets, for refrigerated vans
are practically unheard of.
Meat is carved on wooden
blocks and displayed — unre-
frigerated and uncovered —
in a manner little changed for
centuries.

intertwined with red wool. They are haggling over the price of new red saris for the coming festival season. An older women puffs on a cigarette in the Nepali fashion, drawing the smoke through her cupped fist so the cigarette does not touch her lips. As cigarettes are often shared, this minimizes the risk of passing disease and is common among the elderly and rural folk. The deal is concluded. They tuck their purchases into their bulky cummerbunds — one unfastens her baby from her breast and skilfully wraps it on her back with a red woollen shawl — and they proceed down the old trade route.

I press on, past the shops gleaming with brass and copper cauldrons and water jugs, past a hawker shouldering

a tree of bamboo flutes, skirting a somnolent cow that is blocking traffic. No-one dares to nudge it along, as the fine for maiming or killing a sacred cow is almost as severe as the identical offence against humans, in this, the world's only surviving Hindu kingdom.

A *tap-tap-tap* draws me into a tiny goldsmith's shop in a side alley where an old craftsman is fashioning a hollow gold tube. This is the clasp for a *tilahari*, a necklace made of coloured glass beads worn by Nepali wives. My gaze is drawn by a strange stone which the goldsmith proudly displays. It is fearfully expensive, a cylindrical milky stone with black serpentine markings. Gifted with magnetic qualities these fossilized stones are the auspicious emblem of Vishnu. Fortunate owners dip them in water and drink the sacred liquid while praying to Narayan, as Vishnu is called in Nepal. Known as a *saligram*, these stones only occur in the bed of the Kali

Gandaki gorge, the world's deepest ravine. They are brought along the old trade route to Pokhara and thence to Kathmandu by the clever Thakali people, who monopolize the salt trade between India and Tibet. Saligrams are sought-after and prized by Hindus throughout the sub-continent.

In front of the goldsmith's shop is a Shiva temple whose steps are covered by another valuable commodity from the great trade routes — wool. Draped over the pagoda steps are piles of parrot green and Hindi-red woollen shawls, beside the expensive greys, creams and fawns of the famed pashmina shawls made from the hair of mountain goats, softer and warmer than any others. This is the Indra Chowk, the great wool market of Kathmandu. There is a great commotion as I enter the square, for this is the last day of the Indrajatra festival when the great terrifying mask of Akash Bhairav — a fearsome form of Shiva and guardian deity of Indra Chowk — is displayed in front of his temple. Garlands of marigolds are roped about the ghastly face. Its eyes are forever turned to the heavens, for if his gaze falls to earth,

Left: Shops and stalls are tucked into every niche of Asan Tole, the traditional rice market of Kathmandu. Shop-keepers make use of every available inch of their cramped space even utilizing ceilings for display.

Above: Village girls crowd a roadside stall specializing in hair ornaments, woollen tassels decorated with sequins and bound with silver thread. These are entwined into their hair in a single, long braid, which hangs down their backs.

Above right: Copper and brassware spill onto the pavement in Asan Tole, the busiest intersection in Kathmandu's traditional trading sector.

death and destruction will reign. A group of Nepalese musicians strikes up a mournful dirge, playing on thin brass horns as a priest anoints them with sacred water and marigold petals. The priest ascends a ladder beside the awesome face, the music gains tempo, the horns blare and suddenly . . . rice beer pours forth from the idol's gold-winged mouth. In a wild stampede, the crowd surges forward. The priest collects a terracotta bowl full of beer and sprinkles it over the adoring crowd. A porter lunges to catch the spray and rubs it into his shaven head as the crowd roars its approval, for those who capture some of the sacred liquor receive powerful blessings from the mighty Bhairav. As a finale, the priest sprays the open-mouthed crowd with the last of the beer. Everyone returns to their shops and homes along the old trade route, relieved that the guardian deity has been properly appeased for yet another fiscal year.

CHAPTER 3

Feudal Realms

Kathmandu and the Poet Kings

These young girls seem oblivious to the wrathful Black Bhairav, garlanded with skulls in Kathmandu's Durbar Square. Bhairav, a fierce form of the god Shiva, brandishes weapons in his six arms and tramples on a corpse symbolizing human ignorance. Until recently, this awesome deity was used as a lie detector. Suspects who dared to tell an untruth before it, apparently died while vomiting blood.

Kathmandu. The name alone has a magical ring, conjuring up a place both exotic and wonderful. A name of the same genre as Zanzibar and Casablanca, Zamboanga and Samarkand. Yet for the first 700 years of the city's existence, it was actually known by another name, Kantipur, a most forgettable title. Numerologists claim that names have destinies. If the numerical combination is inauspicious it can affect the fortunes of that person or place. Napoleon, among other luminaries, is said to have changed his name on the advice of a numerologist and his fortunes changed thereafter.

In all fairness, though, Kantipur was a city whose fortunes were already in the ascendant after a most auspicious beginning. Back in the eighth or tenth century, depending which chronicle you read, in the historical era known for obvious reasons as The Dark Ages, a powerful and wealthy potentate by the name of King Gunakamadeva was fasting in honour of Lakshmi, the goddess of wealth. As the story goes, she appeared to him in a dream and directed him to build a city at the sacred junction of the Vishnumati and Bagmati Rivers. Her divine directions were most specific: the city was to be in the form of a curved scimitar, known as a *khadga*; it was to contain 18,000 houses, and everyday 100,000 rupees of business was to be transacted. This benevolent deity promised to reside there herself until those figures had been reached. Business obviously flourished, as the king set about inaugurating festivals and building golden-roofed shrines in his appreciation to the powers that be.

Later, around the 13th century, after a dozen or more kings had come and gone, there appeared on the scene the first of a line of rulers who were to put the city on the map

55

and in the process stamp it indelibly with their mark. These were the Mallas, whose name apparently derives from the Sanskrit meaning "wrestler" or "athlete." According to the ancient chronicles it all came about because King Ari-deva's wife gave birth to a son while he was indulging in his favourite pastime — wrestling.

Malla rule brought a new cultural era to the valley. The arts flourished, trade expanded and except for the odd incursion by outsiders, peace and prosperity reigned. Culture really bloomed during the 15th-century reign of Yaksha Malla, a great patron of the arts but also an empire builder. He expanded Nepal's territories until they stretched from Tibet to Sikkim and down into northern India as far as the Ganges. But Yaksha Malla's main claim to fame, or infamy, was his carving up of the valley into three independent principalities: Kantipur (soon to be Kathmandu), Patan and Bhaktapur. Each city was like a medieval caliphate, ruled by princelings of the Malla dynasty, and bent on outshining one another.

Ratna Malla, the young ruler of Kantipur, got a head start on the others for he had a magic formula in his possession, the sacred mantra of Taleju Bhawani, the Malla clan goddess, whispered by each dying monarch to his chosen son, passed down this way through generations. This essential prescription ensured that the deity would obey all the ruler's commands. To further his alliance with the family goddess, Ratna Malla constructed the soaring, golden-doored, copper-roofed Taleju temple, the highest and most secretive in the valley. Even today, no-one but a few chosen priests know for certain what ceremonies the king, who is an incarnation of Vishnu, performs within its inner chamber.

A century after Ratna Malla, the second miraculous event took place in the city, and Kantipur became known as Kathmandu. As the tale goes, a god known as "The Tree of Paradise" came down from heaven disguised as a mortal to watch the great chariot procession for the Newar deity, Machhendrenath. But he was recognised and imprisoned until he promised to construct with the wood of one tree, a shelter for wandering monks at the crossroads of the great trade routes. The justifiable fame of this miraculous erection gave the city its new name, Kathmandu, which is a colloquial form of the Sanskrit term *kasthamandap* which means "house of wood."

It is still there, tucked away in the nucleus of the old city, but looking much the same as it did eight centuries ago when pilgrims, monks and travelling merchants stayed for the night on its wooden sleeping platforms. During the "flower power" days of the late 1960s and early 70s, hippies used to bed down and smoke hashish here. The hippies have come and gone, but the Kasthamandap hasn't changed, for

the everyday scene is still medieval. A country woman walks in wearing a purple blouse, red sari, silver anklets and with an antique flint box hanging from her waist. She circles the central shrine of Gorakhnath, a deified Shaivite yogi, sprinkles flowers and rice and departs to continue her shopping in the bazaar.

Outside on the steps, a group of barefooted porters sit smoking in the warmth of the winter sun, as I exit into the thicket of temples that is Durbar Square, creation of the Poet King, Pratap Malla. When his insane father died, he was in-capable of passing on the sacred mantra — the key to Malla success — to his son. Doubtless this would have been a giant setback to any lesser man, but Pratap Malla was an extraor-dinary ruler and quickly set about proving that, secret pre-scription or not, he would leave his mark on Kathmandu. He set about constructing bridges and canals, renovating temples and monasteries and even laying a flagstone highway from his city palace to Pashupatinath, Hinduism's holiest Nepal-ese shrine. This ambitious, amorous ruler (he was reputed to have kept 3,000 concubines) built zealously and many of the present day temples and structures in Durbar date from his 17th-century rule.

In a niche above the entrance gate to the Hanuman Dhoka palace, Pratap Malla is immortalised forever in stone, sitting benignly with his queen and flanked by Krishna and a couple of cavorting cowgirls. Painted in rainbow hues, the king and his spouse look rather whimsical and cartoon-like beside the awesome statue of Hanuman, the monkey god, who guards the threshold of the palace which bears his name. Further along the palace wall is a long stone slab inscribed in fifteen languages and a text noting that it was carved under the direction of Pratap Malla, the poet and linguist, in 1664. Legend has it, that if anyone can read all the tongues, milk will pour from the central spout.

Across the way, on the steps of the Jagannath Temple, a saffron-turbanned *sadhu* with a long white beard and creamy-coloured sandalwood paste smeared in stripes across his forehead, settles down against the red pagoda wall. He's renounced the pleasures of the flesh and is oblivious to the sexually explicit scenes carved on the wooden struts above his head. One tableau depicts a woman at a well with her sari at her feet, being surprised by her husband who's snuck up behind her. Other scenes depict a *ménage a tròis* and a dozen or so other diverse sexual activities. But these erotic carvings look comical and artistically crude compared to the graceful gods and goddesses that soar above them. Why they are even here has been a source of much dispute and puzzlement among historians. One theory postulates they were placed here to protect the temples from lightning, as the Lightning Goddess is a virgin and repelled by such scenes. Some say

they attract devotees to the temples. Colin Simpson, in his book *Kathmandu*, evolved a most original theory. He thinks it was a method to encourage population growth. However he adds that "belief in the validity of this explanation was inhibited by the fact that many of the erotic poses depicted were less than likely to result in the production of babies." Others maintain that it depicts the Tantric state of "heavenly bliss" — which is much more likely — for according to Tantric practitioners, pleasure and religious merit are one and the same. They even recommend sexual intercourse as a legitimate means of worship. Most Tantric practises are extremely secret, which probably explains why most Nepalese are unable to elaborate on the real reasons behind the erotic

Left: A bullock ambles unperturbed across the great flagstones of Basantapur square. Its name derives from the lofty pyramidal tower which soars over the palace walls in the background. According to legend, the Malla kings were born on the first floor of the Basantapur Tower; granted audiences on the second; watched dances and pageants from the third; from the fourth floor, the kings would look out over the town before meal times to check that smoke was issuing from every chimney, a sign that food was being cooked and that no households were going hungry.

Right: These mobile fruit-vendors who have ventured up from the Indian plains can set up business anywhere, for their fruit and scales can be packed into woven baskets carried on their heads. They roam about Kathmandu exhorting passers-by to buy their "sweet Kashmiri apples."

carvings. F.D. Colaabavala, writing in *Tantra: The Erotic Cult*, describes a Kathmandu *puja* performed secretly at night in the house of a wealthy devotee when "naked girls wearing jewelled belts and tinkling bells on their hips, their bodies scented and perfumed and their thighs smeared with sandalwood oil, dance gracefully before the male worshippers squattted in a circle." When the energy level has sufficiently aroused the participants, they can blissfully engage in an ecstatic orgy which is fully sanctioned by their ancient texts.

The mystery remains, but for locals it's merely part and parcel of the rich fabric of their lives, interwoven into the culture and religion, unnoticed and indistinguishable. Yet the erotica has disturbed and fascinated Europeans ever since Jesuit priests filtered into the little-known valley in the 17th century. They expressed their disapproval, but their visit raised scarcely a ripple in Malla society. The Newars were too absorbed by their own complex culture and the rivalry and feuding of the three kingdoms. Meanwhile, the Gurkhas were waiting just off stage for their chance to pounce.

Prithvi Narayan Shah, the Gurkha king — whose lineage traced back to the Rajputs of Udaipur — had begun a Napoleon-like takeover of Western Nepal and was obsessed with conquering this rich and fertile valley, the real heart of Nepal. He bided his time while the Mallas kept on with their petty feuding. When a group of Kathmandu dandies came to

Bhaktapur to celebrate the annual New Year festivities, the King of Bhaktapur imprisoned them on the flimsy charge that they were offensively vain in their big-city clothes. So incensed was the king of Kathmandu that he locked up Bhaktapur residents when they came to participate in a religious gathering, and released them only when a hefty ransom had been paid. This was the last straw. The king of Bhaktapur severed diplomatic relations and as punishment he invited the Gurkha king to invade Kathmandu. Privthi Narayan didn't wait for a second chance: his Gurkha warriors descended on the urbane Newars like hungry tigers.

And so the sun set on the Malla dynasty and the gifted Newars lost their independence, but old Kathmandu still remains essentially the creation of these gifted Poet Kings.

Newars, such as these, number more than half of the estimated 800,000 inhabitants of the Kathmandu Valley. Records show that these fun-loving, hospitable and talented people have lived in the valley for at least 2,000 years, and nobody knows for how long before this. They created the unique Nepalese culture, and ruled the Kath-mandu Valley before it was overtaken by the Gurkhas in the 18th century.

Virgin Goddesses

Of all the cultural eccentricities in the Kathmandu Valley none is as bizarre as that of the *kumari*, the living virgin goddess, a Newar girl of the Buddhist faith who is worshipped as a Hindu deity. The Royal Kumari of Kathmandu is the most famous, but there are lesser known kumaris of Patan, Bhaktapur and other valley towns worshipped in the same fashion.

Devotion to virgins began during the valley's early history, but the cult's popularity came of age during the reign of King Jaya Prakash Malla, who inaugurated the annual Kumari Jatra, when a chariot bearing the vestal virgin is pulled through Kathmandu's streets. One story relates that Jaya Prakash Malla used to while away the time playing dice with Taleju, clan goddess of the royal family. On one occasion, she read his lustful thoughts and disappeared. Taleju later reappeared in his dreams, accurately forecast the downfall of the Malla dynasty, and to atone for his sinful thoughts she directed him to select a virgin Newar girl, and to worship her as the goddess Kumari, saying, "for to worship her is to worship me."

Another version, possibly closer to reality, relates that this same king, renowned for his passion for the fairer sex, once made love with a pre-pubescent girl. The youngster died as a result, and this was why Taleju appeared in his conscious-stricken dreams.

A different, but widely believed legend, tells of a Newar girl who claimed to be possessed with the spirit of Taleju. She was banished from the valley, as the king thought she was under an evil influence. After his queen had a fit and announced that Taleju's spirit had entered her body, the king returned the girl to the city. The queen quickly recovered and the young virgin was acclaimed as the Living Goddess Kumari. Her specially built temple, the Kumari Bahal in Kathmandu's Durbar Square, is still the address of the current Royal Kumari, whose life is little changed from that of her divine predecessors.

The selection of kumaris is a zealously guarded Tantric secret, but certain preliminaries discern the most suitable candidates. She must be three or four year old, of the Sakya caste and possess 32 necessary attributes, including unblemished skin, perfect health, shining black hair and a sweet smelling body. Her horoscope must harmonize with the king's. As a final test, she is led through a dark inner chamber of the Hanuman Dhoka where severed buffalo's heads lay about, their eyes ghoulishly lit by candles placed in their horns. Masked demons shriek and leap about her — and if she displays no sign of emotion she is installed as the Living Goddess, for it is believed that any child who exhibits such courage was a superior being in a former life.

When she is adorned in the kumari regalia — her hair bound in a top-knot, a "third eye" painted as a *tikka* on her forehead, dressed in red gowns and ornamented with traditional jewels — the spirit of Kumari is said to enter the young virgin. From this day until her first menstruation, she will be secluded in her palace, only venturing forth on ceremonial occasions like the Indrajatra festival when she places a tikka on the King of Nepal's forehead, thus giving him the right to rule for the coming year. In 1955, the Kumari seemed disoriented when she placed the tikka on Crown Prince Mahendra instead of King Tribhuvan. This was interpreted by seers and astrologers as a most inauspicious sign for the monarch — and he fulfilled the omen by dying eight months later.

CHAPTER 4

Patan

Cradle of the Arts

This masked dancer representing the warrior-god Kaumari performs a solo during the annual dance of the Ashta Matrikas, the eight mother goddesses. To symbolise his role of the "Lord of Battle" he brandishes a khadga, a short sword, and around his neck is a long garland of pale-green barley shoots, the traditional decoration of the Dasain festival.

I f the abundant legends about the valley's most archaic town are true, Patan could well be the oldest Buddhist city in the world. Persistent myths linger that at some time during Gautama Buddha's lifetime, possibly around the dawn of the 6th century BC, the enlightened one visited the valley. It is recounted that during his sojourn in Patan, he raised the blacksmith caste to that of goldsmiths and conferred on them his own name, Sakya, by which this caste is known even today. More tangible evidence of Patan's Buddhist origins is found on the outskirts of the town, where four ancient stupas mark the cardinal points of the ancient city. Numerous chronicles record these were built by Ashoka, the great Buddhist emperor of India, who journeyed to the Kathmandu Valley on a pilgrimage in the footsteps of the Buddha.

Not far from here, where the five-storey pagoda of the Kumbeshwar Temple towers over the surrounding brick townhouses, is the legendary birthplace of Patan, or Lalitpur, as it is also known. The story goes that an ugly, but pious, devotee was gathering herbs here for sale in the market when he was seized by an intense thirst. Finding a nearby pond, he quenched his thirst and bathed. When the devotee returned to town, the Raja happened to meet him and was astonished to see that the formerly ugly herbseller had been transformed into a youth of dazzling beauty. That same night the Raja had a vision which directed him to build on the spot of the miraculous event, a place to be named *Lalita-pattana* — "The Beautiful Town."

Perhaps this title inspired the creators of Patan, for the richly-decorated city houses 55 pagoda temples, and hundreds of lesser shrines and monasteries, all profusely adorned with delicate woodcarvings, bronzes and stone sculpture. Although modern buildings are now encroaching on its traditional *mandala* town plan, the city is still essentially, quite marvellously, archaic. The elegant Durbar Square, with its rich and rare complex of buildings, is the *pièce de résistance*. Historians have given it rave reviews. Percival Landon writes "that as an ensemble, the Durbar Square of Patan possibly remains the most picturesque collection of buildings that has been set in so small a place by the piety and pride of oriental man." And Sylvain Levi, writing in the late 19th century, called it "inconceivably picturesque . . . and in design and composition the noblest of the three," placing it above rivals Kathmandu and Bhaktapur.

A morning mist still blankets the pagoda spires as I walk into the square early one autumn morning. It looks exactly like the old etching in my history book. There are the multi-storied pagodas with their guardian stone elephants, lions and snarling bronze griffins. There is the gilded bronze Malla king kneeling on his lotus plinth atop a lofty stone column, and the graceful colonnaded stone temple with its soaring *shikhara*. Facing all of these is the Royal Palace, made of little pink bricks and adorned with sumptous, wonderful woodwork.

Accordion music drifts down from the Krishna Mandir, the Durbar's stone temple, where early morning worshippers are waking up the gods. Devotees circumambulate the holy shrine, holding brass trays heaped with rice, vermilion powder and marigold petals, ringing bells and rubbing auspicious statues. Opposite, pigeons alight on the upraised hands of the gilded Garuda, atop his stone pillar, where he's been praying for the last 300 years.

Left: Garlanded with ropes of marigolds and wearing a belt of silver rupees over his traditional brocade gown, the guru of the dance awaits the auspicious astrological moment for the ceremony to begin.

Despite the chill in the air, down at the nearby Manga Hiti, a lotus-shaped water conduit, women with brass pots on their heads descend the stone tiers to bathe and collect water which gushes from the stone mouths of *makaras*, mythical crocodiles which look just like the fantastic animals on the gutter spouts of medieval Gothic churches. As I watch a woman cleaning out her brass jug with ashes, a curio seller — who is setting up a display of gleaming *khukri* knives and brass figurines on a nearby pagoda tier — tells me that no-one uses soap here. He said, that if they do, so the old folks say, a giant cobra who dwells in the pipes will get angry and stop the water supply, which apparently runs warm in winter and cold in summer. Townsfolk believe this water, and that from the sacred well of the Kumbeshwar Temple, originates from holy Gosainkunda Lake, high in the mountains, and it flows through subterranean streams to Patan. Every year on the occasion of Janai Purnima, the festival when Brahmins don their new sacred thread, thousands make the arduous pilgrimage to the 5,000-meter-high lake.

The Newars, with their advanced terraced agriculture, have always been masters of irrigation, engineering brilliant water systems centuries ago which directed liquid from mountain streams to flow along stone channels right into the heart of their heavily populated cities and towns. One of the most famed of these ancient water works is the marvellous Tusa Hiti, known as the Royal Bath, in the south courtyard of the Royal Palace. Every surface of this stone masterpiece is elaborately carved, with niches full of gods and goddesses which the king prayed to after his bath. A large, double-headed stone serpent coils its way around the rim to rest its stony gaze on a jaunty Hanuman, the monkey god,

Above: The Dance of the Ashta Matrikas is performed for nine nights in front of Patan's Krishna Mandir Temple and on the tenth night in the Mul Chowk courtyard of the Patan Royal Palace.

Right: A young dancer, his head wrapped in protective cloth, solemnly awaits the dance with a dahlia-bedecked, mother-goddess mask on his lap.

69

Bhairav, the god of terror,
with his long matted hair and
wearing a blue mask and
robes, leads the eight mother
goddesses as they swirl about
the courtyard in their
frenzied dance, accompanied
by blasting horns and the
chanting of ancient texts.

sheltered under a brass umbrella. In front of him is a square stone block, like a king-sized bed, which bears a sign directing tourists not to sit on it, for this was where the regal presence carried out his daily meditations.

In this same palace, on the tenth day of the great Dasain festival, the celebrated Ramayana time when the forces of virtue triumph over evil, I chance upon a most intriguing and fascinating spectacle. Drawn along with a milling crowd of Nepalese families, I find myself in the midst of an expectant throng in the Mul Chowk courtyard of the Royal Palace. Here, but once a year, is staged the masked dance of the Ashta Matrikas, the eight mother goddesses.

I find a spot beside a pert-breasted, brass statue of the Goddess Jamuna who, with her sister Ganga, guards the entrance to the secret shrine of Taleju. In the centre is a man with a shaven head, wearing a gathered brocade skirt and a tight-sleeved bodice – this is the dance guru. Children sit on the brass crocodile and tortoise that support the deities. Beside me and the curvaceous Ganga, a man skins the head of a water buffalo which has just been sacrificed. Blood lays in puddles on the courtyard bricks and is smeared over the beaten brass doors of the shrine just inches from my back. Overhead, draped about a brass *torana* depicting the Ashta Matrikas is a twirling balloon. I realise later, on closer inspection, that it's a length of buffalo's intestine. The smell of blood, sweat and marigolds is pervasive, but there is little time to dwell on my odorous situation for the players arrive.

One by one, a dozen slender young male dancers appear. They have spent the morning meditating at the shrine of the particular goddess that each represents, and that is why they turn up singly and not en masse. Wearing

71

heavy silver ornaments and the same ancient Newar dress of their guru — but of different coloured brocades — they sit on chairs in a circle while assistants help them to wind long lengths of white cotton about their heads and necks. This is to protect their sensitive, newly-shaved heads from the masks, which they now hold in their laps. These weird, colourful masks are carved and painted to represent each of the eight mother goddesses and the other four accompanying deities.

A one-eyed musician fits together a slender brass horn, the drummers stub out their cigarettes and take their positions as the masks are lowered. With this action the spirit of the deity enters the dancers, for there is a special, blessed nut hidden in a pocket of each mask which invites a trance.

Left: When the dance-guru dons his mask, he has taken on the form of Varahi, the sow-faced mother goddess who represents the power to eliminate envy. Each of his hand actions and body movements has great symbolism for the initiated Tantric practitioner.

Right: As the other tranced dancers await their turn in the background, a young male dancer takes on the form of the evil Chamunda, one of the eight mother goddesses.

As the spirits take possession, the dancer's legs begin a strange, palsied shaking which sets their ankle bells jingling. Gongs are beaten, copper horns blast forth and a group of men sing a dirge, reading from a manuscript of ancient Newari script. The air is electric. An old two-metre-long *paubha* — a religious painting on cloth, this one depicting the "Lord of Dance" — is unfurled and held in front of the dancers by two young boys. The dancers move with rigid, trance-like movements, solo and in groups, to a backdrop of weird music. Then, with a wild flurry of horns, they jump to their feet for a feverish finale.

As the masks are removed, the dancers stop shaking, for with their sacred identity removed, the trance is finished. The ancient dance of the Ashta Matrikas has been performed for yet another year in Patan, the cultural heartland of the Kathmandu Valley.

CHAPTER 5

Bhaktapur
Return to the Middle Ages

By October, the rice harvest is in full swing along the old trade route into Bhaktapur. Golden grain is spread to dry in the autumn sunshine and farmer's wives, wearing homespun black saris with red hems, winnow the harvested rice using shallow baskets.

As I bicycle along the road to Bhaktapur, the countryside is toned in shades of orange and red. The poplars are losing their leaves, and when the wind comes up they drift down like bronze confetti. Their pencil-straight trunks throw long shadows across the avenue. The harvest is nearly in, and the fields are spread with fan-shaped sheaves of drying straw. Pillars of golden corn and haystacks shaped like conical African huts are scattered about the terraced fields that rise from the river in scalloped tiers.

It has been almost two decades since I last saw Bhaktapur and I wonder if it will be the same medieval town I walked through all those years ago? There were no lodges then, no restaurants, just a tea-house, where by the light of a kerosene lamp we made the acquaintance of a government clerk who spoke a few words of English. "You must stay the night with my guru," he insisted, leading us down a dark maze of cobblestoned streets to a riverside temple and the tiny room of his spiritual guide. There atop a tiger's skin, dreadlocks piled about his head, clad only in a lioncloth, sat a Shaivite *sadhu* with the most intense gaze I have yet to behold. He clapped his hands and three women, wrapped in blankets at his feet, woke up and scurried out the door. He motioned us to take their place and, as the government clerk bent and kissed his feet, the guru stuffed ganja — the resinous Nepalese marijuana — into a chillum pipe. Lord Shiva's name was evoked before smoking, for this is a plant heartily enjoyed by the Great Destroyer and Creator, and his ardent disciples fervently follow his example. Smoke filled the room, his eyes grew brighter and more intense, and I fell asleep at the sadhu's feet . . . so long ago.

I am struck by a sense of deja-vu at the little

conifer-clad hill just before town, as if I have come across a scene from a vivid recurring dream. Oblique shafts of sunlight filter through the pines. Nearby, black cattle graze with white egrets perched on their backs. Jyapu women, of the farmer caste, wearing their characteristic black saris with red hems, sway down the road with brass water jugs balanced on their hips. Men loaded with hay trudge uphill, like walking haystacks. The road skirts a large pond where women slap their washing against stones. Then it narrows into a brick lane walled with old townhouses, and eventually terminates at a pair of snarling stone lions who sit on their haunches guarding the entrance to Durbar Square. We have arrived.

Historically, Bhaktapur is not as old as either Patan

In the canyon-like streets of Bhaktapur, where houses can be four storeys high, the winter sun only penetrates for a few hours a day. These Newar men (left), taking a break from work, make the most of the sunshine, as do the women and their young daughters (above), prettied-up for a festive occasion.

or Kathmandu. But oddly enough it looks older, for the city has managed to preserve its medieval identity almost intact. There are no modern buildings, nothing obtrusive that jars the eye. The russet-brick houses with their sumptuous woodwork, the brick-paved streets and squares with their pagodas and temples, the low-roofed, open-front shops and the traditional markets all complement each other in a most aesthetic way.

Bhaktapur has always been apart, aloof and more self-sufficient than her sister city states. Historians record that while anarchy raged in Kathmandu and Patan, Bhaktapur remained the seat of stable dynasties. Even when the Gurkhas conquered the valley in the 18th century, Bhaktapur suffered less, for the inhabitants succumbed to treason and never underwent a seige. Perhaps this is why the city has managed to stay so uniquely intact.

Some things have changed though. A glance at a 19th-century etching shows that formerly, Durbar Square was

Above: Porters trudge along a Bhaktapur street, carting loads that anywhere else in the world would require a small truck. In the Kathmandu Valley, human labour is still cheap and plentiful. Not only are vehicles rare and expensive, but many of the valley's trails and tracks are so steep that porters will have ample work for many years to come. This hardly concerns an old Bhaktapur resident (right), in loose jodhpur pants, inhaling a draught of tobacco smoke from his hookah.

cluttered with temples and pagodas, quite different from today's open space. This was the shattering result of the great earthquake of 1934 that ruined many of Bhaktapur's multi-storied temples and destroyed hundreds of other buildings. Despite this, the effect is still magnificent.

A golden figure of Bupathindra, the 17th-century Malla king who gave Bhaktapur most of its famous buildings, sits atop a pillar, shaded by an imperial umbrella, gazing at his former home and creation, the Palace of 55 Windows, each one a tribute to Newar woodcarving. Directly opposite is the marvellous creation of a later ruler, Jaya Ranjit, the last of the Malla line. The Sun Dhoka, or Golden Gate, is by common consent, the greatest work of art in the entire valley and is a fitting memorial to the late, great Mallas. Set into a wall of tiny glazed terracotta bricks, this gleaming portal — with its multi-armed goddess, glaring garuda, writhing serpents, prancing lions and bellowing elephants — is actually modelled in copper and coated with a gilding that has a proportion of gold.

In a courtyard on the inside of the golden portal, in front of the sacred Taleju Temple, a group of girls in burgundy-coloured saris and black blouses, with jasmine flowers twisted into their braids, are picking dirt and grime from a pile of antique wooden pillars. Under a nearby pavilion, Newar craftsmen chisel at a block of *sal*, a prized timber that most of the valley's ornate woodwork is fashioned from. They are carving a replica of an old *torana*, the semi-circular crests which appear over the doors of religious sanctums. This, and the pillars the girls are cleaning, are to be used in the West German-assisted reconstruction of a pagoda which was destroyed in the great earthquake.

Down a back lane in Bhaktapur, the local barber shaves a
customer, one of the potters
from the adjacent pottery
market. He works under a
portico supported by deli-
cately-carved wooden col-
umns, open to the street and
its sights and sounds.

80

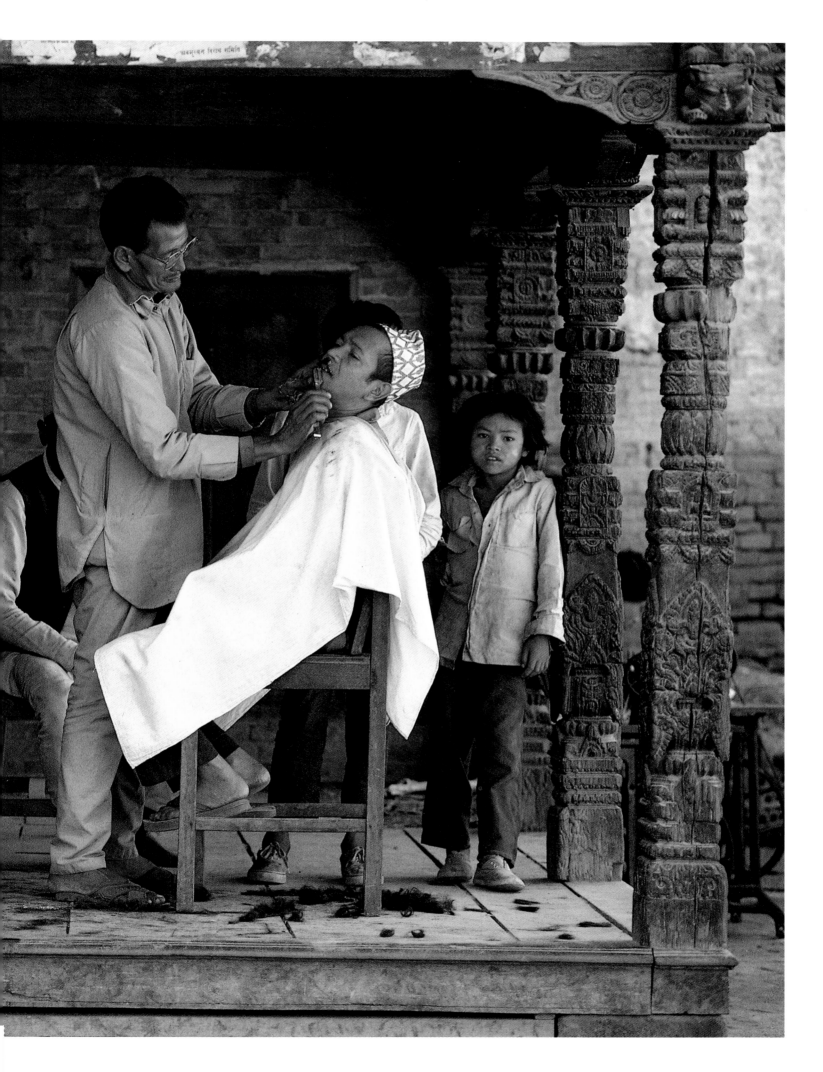

Outside, under a brilliant blue sky, a crowd is gathering in a brick-paved corner of the square, where a travelling medicine man is warming up for his performance. Bhaktapur reminds me of those early traveller's tales that describe the strange and exotic bazaars of Asia, for there is always some bizarre event taking place in the streets. With a three-metre long python draped around his neck, the medicine man strolls the periphery of the crowd, swinging the reptile closer to the audience. Everyone screams and retreats and then laughingly regroups for a better look. All the while the showman strokes the snake's cream-coloured belly and exhorts the crowd to buy his cure-all ointment, which has some magical reptilian ingredient. His performance also involved a mongoose with a bell around its neck and a cobra.

The show over, I amble on. Past a shop full of shining brassware and a man hawking cages of green parrots with red beaks. Past a sweet musky smell that envelopes an old Newar man puffing on a large ceramic hookah, into a spacious paved square dominated by the five-storey Nyatapola, the tallest temple in the Kathmandu Valley. Flanking the steep staircase that mounts the temple's approach are a host of stone giants, elephants, lions, griffins and goddesses — each of these thought to be ten times stronger than the one beneath. On the lowest tier, beside a pair of giant turban-clad Malla wrestlers, a group of dark-skinned men thump kapok through a sieve and then stuff it into bolsters and quilts. These are seasonal quiltmakers who journey up from the Terai for the coming cold season. They wander through the streets and lanes, plucking a strange bass note on their wooden instruments and extolling householders to order their quilts before the cold weather sets in.

A pungent spicy aroma fills the adjoining square, where shiny red chillies dry on rattan mats. Washing flutters from bamboo poles protruding from ornately carved windows, as a woman strips to the waist and massages mustard oil into her shoulders and breasts. Down a few more lanes I emerge at the pottery market, where in a large open square, hundreds of black and ochre terracotta wares dry in the October sun. There are round black pots and ones with spouts in the shape of tiny elephants, bulbous water vessels and large pottery tubs known as *attals*, in which townswomen do their washing. Plastic has yet to make a dent in Bhaktapur's traditions. Under the verandah of an old carved portico, a potter heaps a pile of clay onto a large flat wheel which he sets in motion with a long stick, dextrously turning out another pot. Later, the pottery will be fired in the age-old way by stacking straw over a mound of pots and lighting it.

Every town still has its own potters, who form a distinct caste known as *Kumhars*, and at Bhaktapur they are renowned for the production of black terracotta. Rows of these wares are spread in the sunny courtyard. When dry they are put back on the potter's wheel and rubbed smooth with a piece of horn which gives them their characteristic shiny surface. The black colour is produced during firing, when air inlets in the straw pile are plugged. The smoke can't escape, so carbon particles build up and coat the pottery its distinctive dark hue. One remarkable fact about the pottery market is that everything is made for the sole use of local folk, unlike many other parts of the world where traditional arts and crafts only exist for the tourist trade.

Bhaktapur maintains an aura of self sufficiency: the surrounding fields produce the town's rice; the bricks for houses and streets are made from the local clays; even roof tiles are handmade in the vicinity. And this is what gives Bhaktapur its unique integrated feeling.

Above: The pyramid-shaped Nyatapola Temple — at over 30 metres, Nepal's tallest temple — towers over the ochre-coloured skyline of Bhaktapur.

Right: Seated on a stone
pedestal, a gilded King
Bupathindra Malla overlooks
Bhaktapur's Durbar Square.

CHAPTER 6

Gurkhas and God-Kings

A turn-of-the-century, hand-tinted studio portrait shows Prime Minister Chandra Sumsher Jung Bahadur Rana in full regalia. The Ranas held power for a century, during which they kept the Shah kings prisoners in their own palaces. Chandra Sumsher was alleged to have led the puppet king into a life of debauchery, but the British gave him a knighthood for abolishing the Hindu rite of suttee.

From its perch on a rocky hilltop, a few miles southwest of Kathmandu, the fortified village of Kirtipur commands a sweeping view of the entire valley. It is easy to see why this was the site of the heroic last stand by the Mallas against the Gurkhas, for their other settlements lay on lower ground and were easy targets for invaders. Kirtipur, installed on its perpendicular rock in a seemingly impregnable situation, valiantly repelled the invaders on their first attempt, but the Gurkhas returned later with heavy reinforcements and overcame the town. In retaliation for his initial failure and the stoic resistance of the Newars, the Gurkha king, Prithvi Narayan Shah, ancestor of the present ruling family, ordered his army to amputate the noses of every male in Kirtipur, excluding those who could play wind instruments. Perhaps this is why one biographer describes the Gurkha monarch as, "dispassionately barbarous and generous after mature deliberation."

Twenty-five years later, an Englishman, Colonel Kirkpatrick, led an East India Company force to aid the Gurkhas in their war against Tibet. They arrived too late, for the skirmish was over, but he saw the results of the Kirtipur disfiguration firsthand. "We came to the knowledge of this fact in consequence of observing among the porters who transported our baggage over the hills, a remarkable number of noseless men, the singularity of the circumstances leading us to inquire into the cause of it."

Two centuries have softened the memory. All that is left as a tangible reminder, are dozens of lethal curved *khukri* knives nailed on the walls of Kirtipur's Bagh Bhairav Temple. Weapons left by the victorious Gurkhas the day the village fell. Somehow, a gloom still pervades the decaying town. The

85

inhabitants are not as houseproud or jolly as those of Bhakta-pur and other towns. There is a degenerate atmosphere, a sense of neglect. A high school student complains bitterly to me that they must still study in Nepali, the language of the conquerors. His own tongue, Newari, is not encouraged. The emotional scars remain.

Prithvi Narayan's statue at the centre of the village depicts him as the noble "Founder of the Nation" and history books tactfully glorify his bloody conquests, for his heirs still hold power in this Himalayan kingdom, even though they lost it for over a century to their arch rivals — the Ranas.

Jung Bahadur Rana, the usurper of the Shah kings, was an amazing character, even allowing for the fact that many of the historians who portrayed him so favourably were actually working during his reign. Despite his bloody rise to power, he was depicted as the "new-mannered Gurkha" with an acutely discerning mind. Never mind the fact he was illit-erate. Carrying on the traditions of the Gurkhas, who unlike the Newars, were indifferent patrons of arts and letters, Jung Bahadur's physical prowess was legendary. It was said he could pirouette on horseback while riding across an abyss on a plank, tackle tigers armed only with a khukri, and that once he spent an entire day hanging by his nails to the inside of a well, where he'd been left for dead by an arch rival.

The time was ripe for a takeover, for Prithvi Nar-ayan's heirs were a worthless bunch. As one historian put it, they were "connected more to pathology than to history; they are degenerates of various types, nervous, irritable, san-guinary, impulsive, alcoholic, erotic and idiots . . . A long series of minorities leaves the child king in the dreadful hands of a mother, or of a minister, jealous of the throne and

Big game hunting was the favourite sport of the Nepal-ese nobility until the mid-20th century, and the Terai — the lowland jungle region that borders India — was famous for its tigers and rhinos. After the "beat" (above right), sportsmen such as Colonel Chandra Jung Thapa (above left) and King Tribhuvan (bottom right) would find the game an easy mark. As a result, very few large animals remain today and these are highly protected.

interested in prolonging the child's complete exhaustion by precocious debaucheries."

The shrewd and opportunistic Jung Bahadur rose through the ranks of the army, ingratiating himself to those in power. Even the British Resident mentions that he was most intelligent, an expert in military matters and, "though young in years profoundly versed in intrigue." It wasn't long before he made use of this gift. Goaded by the doltish king and one of his lesser queens, Jung Bahadur shot his uncle, the prime minister, and was rewarded with the title of general. Encouraged by this success he purged the rest of his rivals in a bloody massacre at the Kot Courtyard in Kathmandu's Durbar Square. Figures vary widely on the number of ministers and nobles who were gunned down on that gory evening in 1846. Official records name 55 but the real toll was more like 500.

Blood still flowed through the gutters the day I visited the Kot Courtyard, for true to form, this is the scene of the army's annual bloodbath for the Dasain festival, when scores of buffalo and goats are sacrificed. Regimental standards fluttered over piles of newly-severed animal heads draped with garlands of marigolds. A Gurkha raised his glinting blade over a buffalo tied to a stake, and with one stroke the head tumbled to the ground, accompanied by a volley of gunshots. The regimental band struck up an eccentric carnival-type tune while the carcass was dragged about the tiles, leaving blood in a circle about the standards, the heads and other ritual offerings. If the Gurkha fails to lop off the beast's head in one swoop — a prodigious feat even with a carefully honed *khora* (a larger version of the *khukri*) — the regiment is disgraced and it bodes ill for the year ahead. The day I

watched, everything went according to plan. Heads rolled and blood flowed in the Kot Courtyard. Jung Bahadur Rana would have felt at home.

As soon as he had installed himself as Nepal's undisputed ruler, with the puppet-king safely under lock and key, Jung Bahadur and a huge retinue set sail for Europe where he was acclaimed as the "lion of the Paris and London season." He returned to Nepal with his prestige doubled. But not everyone was impressed with his globe-trotting. The powerful Brahmin priests declared that he had lost caste by eating with Europeans and was therefore unfit to rule a Hindu kingdom. But Jung Bahadur smelt a rat, quickly ascertaining that it was a plot to have him dethroned, and he exiled the intriguers to India. His sojourn in civilized Europe had obviously tempered the Rana, for not so long ago he wouldn't have hesitated to put the offenders to the sword. A new, mock-European era began.

The Ranas set about emulating the grandeur of Europe's baroque palaces and courtly life. It was now passe to live in the medieval palaces built by the Newars, and the nobles and aristocrats embarked on an ambitious building spree, constructing stucco colonnaded palaces — eclectic combinations of Greek, Roman, English and Indian styles.

The most ostentatious was the 1700-room Singha Durbar, the prime minister's residence, but there were hundreds more. Among these was the elegant Versailles-style palace of Field Marshall Kaiser Shumsher, which housed the largest private library in the Orient. When the Ranas were ousted from power, many of the nobles fled and their palaces fell to rack and ruin, or were appropriated as government offices, denuded of their grandeur. The Kaiser's palace was

After engineering a massacre of his opponents, stern-faced Jung Bahadur Rana (far right) seized power in 1846. His family ruled until they were ousted by King Tribhuvan, the rightful Shah ruler, in 1951. Tribhuvan is pictured (far left) as a youth, still powerless under autocratic Rana rule.

spared this fate, for even though part of the complex is now a ministry, the library — his *raison d'etre* — is intact. It's like a Rana museum, or a page from one of his own history books. Kaiser Shumsher was also known as an oriental Talleyrand, for this shrewd, highly intelligent man (it is said that he read every book in his vast collection) survived many a palace intrigue. Even after the downfall of the Ranas he continued to receive honours and titles from the reinstalled Shah kings.

Nowadays you can find the Kaiser's library behind a high brick wall, surrounded by lush gardens where birds chirp in the rhododendron bushes and screeching fruit bats hang upside down from the *bunya* pines. Inside you cannot hear the bats, nor much of anything but thumbs on pages: it's a haven of peace and quiet away from the noise of the streets and the hustle of the local salesman. In the reading room, Nepali men sit buried in newspapers beneath a pastel-hued and curlicued ceiling. All about the walls are great maps of the world with obsolete empires marked in gold lettering. Framed between two huge mounted globes, one terrestrial and the other celestial, a large stuffed tiger appears to pace the marble floor. Bookcases line the walls, and above these are the ubiquitous, larger-than-life oils of Shah kings in full ceremonial dress, presiding over an odd empire of artefacts — a rhino skull, suits of armour and a wild buffalo's head with a two-metre hornspan. Scattered about are smaller paintings of writers, poets and historians, intimates of the late Kaiser who, it is said, possessed an encyclopedic memory of his collection and could quote from any book at random. A gold-leafed staircase mounts the second floor where Ranas gaze out from oils and early hand-tinted colour photographs. Light streams through French windows. Here, lining the

After Jung Bahadur Rana returned from his maiden trip to London and Paris in 1850, things European came into vogue. The nobility sat for studio portraits, and the women fashioned skirts by joining saris together. Historian Daniel Wright relates that "the ladies of the higher classes like their muslin to be sixty or eighty yards in length. Of course they cannot walk much with such a bundle round them."

walls, is a photographic history of Rana rule. Family portraits, visits of foreign dignitaries, young nobles lounging by automobiles, tiger shoots and more tiger shoots. For this was the sport of kings and the jungles of Nepal's Terai region were among the most famed of shooting venues.

Although Nepal was strictly out of bounds for foreign visitors, a notable exception was made for British royalty, great devotees of bloodsports. Yet they were only invited as far as the Terai; mysterious Kathmandu was still off limits. For King George V's shoot, 600 elephants were mustered for "the beat" to trap tigers and other game. His Britannic Majesty bagged 21 tigers, ten rhinos and two bears, and in gratitude showered his host, Chandra Shamsher, with a prestigious title, 2,000 rifles and five million rounds of ammunition. A tale which circulated after that regal shoot tells of King George and Queen Mary's flush toilet, which was never connected to a water supply. Each time a royal presence pulled the chain, a servant stationed at a spyhole would throw a bucket of water down the pipe. Plumbing was, and still remains, a rather mysterious art in Nepal.

In later years, King Mahendra upstaged the Ranas and put on an even more grandiose shoot for Queen Elizabeth II. There were even "bar elephants" which circulated among the mounted guests serving iced champagne. Prince Philip turned up sporting a bandaged "trigger" finger, which word tells was an excuse not to partake of any shooting himself, for in 1961 concern for the world's vanishing wildlife was just starting to make itself heard. This didn't overly concern Lord Home, who bagged one of Nepal's last one-horned rhinos. The Queen also showed little worry as she tucked into a spread of 22 wildlife dishes.

Surprisingly, it was a hunting party that sealed the fate of the century-old Rana rule. King Tribhuvan, the powerless puppet ruler, imprisoned in his palace like a bird in a gilded cage, seemed to be the least likely candidate for revolution. Perhaps that's why — as he drove off with his family on a leopard hunt, the Shah jewels hidden in picnic baskets — his Rana jailers didn't suspect a thing. Until the royal limousines swung through the gates of the Indian Embassy and into political asylum. Three months later, under pressure from India and the populace, the Ranas stepped down. King Tribhuvan, direct descendant of the Gurkha Shah kings, Incarnation of Vishnu, Divine Emperor and Five Times Godly returned from exile in triumph. Ranarchy was no more, but the new monarchy was just as ostentatious.

When King Mahendra, Tribhuvan's son, was crowned in 1955, Nepal opened its doors. The international media looked in for the first time, to witness a pageant the likes of which had never been seen by the outside world. On a silver howdah, shaded by a golden umbrella, the king rode on elephant back to the old royal palace in the heart of Kathmandu. Here he was daubed with mud from the elephant's stables to give him strength and Himalayan clay to impart wisdom. Priests anointed him with sacred waters, milk, curd and *ghee*, then raised him to the golden throne which stood on the skins of a tiger, leopard, ox and cat, symbolising the monarch's sovereignty over all creatures. It was whispered that in previous coronations there was an additional skin, that of a human. To the whir of the cine cameras, at the exact minute of the astrologer's calculations, the crown — fringed with emeralds as large as pigeon's eggs and topped with a metre-long plume from a New Guinea Bird of Paradise — was lowered onto the God-King's head. Kathmandu had made its debut on the world stage.

Pomp and pageantry was part of everyday life during the Rana's 104-year reign. Huge baroque palaces were built, rulers wore crowns with emeralds as large as bird's eggs, great hunts were organized for visiting royalty, but they alienated themselves from the general population, who lived a feudal existence until the Second World War. Above: King Tribhuvan as a boy with his Rana jailers. Far right: Prime Minister Juddha Shumsher. Near right: Prime Minister Bir Shumsher Rana.

In 1661, Fathers Grueber and Dorville, Jesuit priests stationed at Beijing, received a papal order to return to Europe, but as Dutch fleets were blockading the Chinese ports they were left with no option but to travel overland, and so became the first Europeans to venture into Nepal. No doubt, they would not have embarked on their trip without some prior knowledge of the route, and it is quite probable they had heard of Father Andrada, an adventurous monk, who had, forty years earlier, passed the source of the Ganges, crossed the high Tibetan passes and founded a church at Chaprang. During his two-year sojourn in Tibet, Father Andrada met with Nepalese artisans who had emigrated there, commenting that "the King of this place (Chaprang) has three or four goldsmiths, natives of a place separated from here by two months of marching and subjugated to two kings, each one individually more powerful than this one, but of the same religion." The craftsmen were undoubtedly Newars and their homeland Nepal.

Grueber and Dorville, those unsung heroes of Asian exploration, travelled from Beijing to Lhasa, where they stopped for two months, and then continued to India — via Nepal. Grueber briefly comments that "Nepal abounds in all things that are necessary for the sustenance of life." Other missionaries followed, but it was a trickle, not a torrent.

The Malla rulers were tolerant of different faiths. Not so the Gurkhas, who took their place. When King Prithvi Narayan Shah conquered the Kathmandu Valley in 1768, he expelled the missionaries, who it is said destroyed thousands of ancient Nepalese manuscripts in revenge. The Gurkhas firmly closed the country's doors once again, declaring that "the tradesman brings the Bible, the Bible brings the bayonet."

Ironically, the Gurkhas probably wouldn't have subdued the Mallas as quickly if it hadn't been for the European merchants who supplied them with firearms that tipped the balance of power in their favour. Despite the Gurkha dislike of foreigners, when they were having difficulties with the Chinese in 1790 they asked the English — busy consolidating themselves in India — to assist, adding the possibility of a commercial treaty as enticement.

When Colonel William Kirkpatrick and his troops arrived in Nepal — the first Englishmen to penetrate "The Forbidden Valley" — they discovered they were too late. The Gurkhas had balked on the idea of a treaty of commerce, alarmed that it would threaten their independence, and they had hastily concluded a peace treaty with China. Although Kirkpatrick was received with indifference, he inaugurated a new phase of European expansion. He was one of that rare breed of men peculiar to the Age of Discovery, who possessed not only leadership qualities, but also a keen sense for geography, history, antiquities, religion, agriculture and commerce. Kirkpatrick recorded his observations in a prodigiously entitled book, *An Account of the Kingdom of Nepal* — being the substance of observations made during a mission to that country, in the year 1793.

The colonel eventually signed a commercial treaty with the Gurkhas and he lists the "Exports to the Com-

pany's and Vizier's Dominions" as "Elephants, Elephants teeth, Rice of kinds, Timber of sorts, Hides of sorts, Ginger, Kuth or Terra japonica (white or black), Turmeric, Wax, Honey, Behroza (or pure resin of the pine), Walnuts, Oranges, Long Pepper, Long Pepper root, Ghee, Teigh (or aromatic bark of the root of the bastard cinnamon), Taiz-pat (dried leaf of ditto), Large Cardamons, Roal or dammer, Lamp-Oil and Cotton (of the Simul tree)."

On the strength of this treaty, a British Resident arrived in the Kathmandu Valley in 1802, but he left barely a year later complaining that little could be accomplished

The First Explorers

Head of the Kustoora or Musk Deer.

with a people "amongst whom no engagements, however solemnly contracted, are considered binding." Relations between the two powers deteriorated and, in 1814, Britain declared war on the Gurkhas, saying they were disgusted with the Gurkha's bad faith and constant marauding into Indian territory. The British, unaccustomed to the terrain, suffered disastrous failures at first. But eventually, after two years of defeats and victories on each side, the Gurkhas were forced into a peace treaty, under which they relinquished part of the Terai region. The British forces, however, never got as far as the Kathmandu Valley. The enigma remained.

A British Resident was reluctantly allowed to return, yet his movements were restricted to the Kathmandu Valley, and apart from one assistant and a personal physician, no other Europeans were allowed to enter Nepal. Diplomatically emasculated, the Resident was forced to make the best of a rather odd job. He was given land in a malaria-infested, unhealthy part of the valley, said to be barren and haunted. Yet the British, with their stubborn persistance, turned it into a little corner of England, with an abundant garden that supplied European vegetables.

CHAPTER 7

A Pantheon of Gods

This *sadhu*, a wandering ascetic, finds a temple step a
handy spot for a rest in
Patan's Durbar Square. He is
a Shaivite, a follower of the
great Hindu god, Shiva, and is
characterized by his dreadlocks, necklace of sacred
rudraksha seeds and saffron-
coloured garments. Hun-
dreds of sadhus make the
long pilgrimage from the
plains of India every year for
the Shiva Ratri festival.

They are found crowning the hilltops, hugging
the banks of holy streams, sheltered in cliffside
caves, and scattered amongst the rice terraces.
In the Kathmandu Valley, it has often been
said that temples and shrines outnumber the
houses. There are great gilded pagoda-style
temples, colossal white-domed stupas with their strange "all-
seeing eyes" and hundreds of smaller Buddhist *chaityas*.
There are wayside temples guarded by carved animals, sacred
stones daubed with red powder sunk into crowded streets,
blood-stained sacrificial shrines, and multitudes of tiny altars
nestled under sacred trees, beside mountain springs and
tucked into niches in almost every valley home.

Daniel Wright, the historian, estimated that in the
19th century there were 2,733 shrines and temples in the
Kathmandu Valley, and that wasn't counting private households. There is no reason to believe this figure has lessened,
for religion is still the essence of Nepalese existence, and the
rhythms of the ancient lunar calendar, calculated by astrologer priests, still dictate the annual flow of festivals which
mark the changing seasons and pay homage to the multitudes of gods and goddesses.

In this valley, religion is interwoven in people's lives.
Temples reflect this attitude. For along with all the constant
comings and goings of devotees there are dozens of other
activities enacted in and around the temple precincts.
Hawkers display their vegetables, woollens and curios, porters wait for customers, crops are spread to dry, children play
hide-and-seek, sadhus and other wandering ascetics may
even build temporary shelters. Animal life is prolific; sacred
cows at the temple steps shadowing the vegetable stalls, dogs
guarding the food offerings at the shrine, and always

97

monkeys, frisking about the eaves and swinging from the pagoda roofs.

Hinduism has, as one ancient text boasts, 300 million deities. A staggering number, even when one considers that each god can have countless names and appear in a myriad of different forms; male, female, neuter, animate or inanimate. And in a variety of aspects; kind, generous, loving, benevolent or ferocious and bloodthirsty. However what really complicates this devotional scene is that along with all the Hindu gods there are also the holy Buddhas, countless bodhisattvas and the unique hybrid gods of both these religions that appear only in Nepal. Like Machhendrenath, the much worshipped god of the Newars, the great rain-

Worshippers gather early each morning on the *ghats* at Pash-upatinath Temple, Nepal's holiest Hindu site. Devotees believe that locked within the sacred womb of the temple are the fabulous treasures of Lord Shiva, guarded by an awesome snake god known as Basuki Naga. Those who come to pray to Shiva must first do obeisance to the snake god, whose temple stands next door.

maker and ruler and protector of the Kathmandu Valley.

Originally, like all ancient peoples, the valley dwellers were animists. They worshipped the sun and moon, the great mountains that soared above them, the sustaining rivers, the forests where game abounded, and auspicious rocks, trees and springs where natural spirits dwelt. Fertility worship and devotion to ancestors was intertwined with early religion and many of the magical arts and skills needed to ensure health, prolong life, make children, exorcise evil spirits and destroy one's enemies, evolved during prehistoric times. Much of this still survives, absorbed and blended with the later introductions of Buddhism and Hinduism.

According to Newar tradition, Buddhism was the first great religion to reach the Kathmandu Valley. Archaeological evidence proves this a historical certainty. Hinduism arrived later, in the fifth century AD, and it is said that the Licchavi rulers adopted this new religion under the influence of their powerful relatives, the Gupta emperors of

India. The Licchavis favoured Vishnu, the second of the Hindu triad, the great preserver and protector, and many of the ancient Narayan (his Nepali name) temples that abound in the valley were constructed at this time. However, it wasn't long before the Shiva cult was established in the protected vale, and by the seventh century it dominated Nepalese Hinduism.

Lord Shiva is adored as the Great God, the Destroyer and Creator. He is the brooding, long-haired ascetic, his loins girded with animal skins, his ash-smeared body garlanded with snakes and brandishing his trademark, the three-pronged trident. One of his many manifestations is Pashupathi, Protector of Animals, and his temple Pashupati-

Left: Machhendrenath, believed to be the most compassionate divinity in the valley, is worshipped by both Hindus and Buddhists even though it is a Buddhist god.

nath, on the outskirts of Kathmandu beside the Bagmati River, is one of Hinduism's most hallowed shrines.

Even on a misty winter's morning, the faithful congregate at the *ghats* of the riverside temple. Women in clinging wet saris emerge from the cold waters of the sacred stream after their purifying post-menstruation bath. A sadhu takes the plunge, dressed only in a G-string. The lingam — a stone phallic symbol — Shiva's symbol at the water's edge, is kept constantly wet by devotee's ablutions. Bells ring from inside the walled temple complex, accessible only to Hindus, where *pujas* are performed in front of a great golden bull who guards the sacred womb of the gilded triple-roofed temple. Here is the holiest of all lingams. Each year, thousands flock to watch priests douse the phallic idol with its annual bath of cow's milk, yoghurt, honey, sugar, clarified butter and holy water. It is then anointed with sandalwood,

Above: A silver image of Ganesh, the elephant-headed god, is visited by people embarking on a journey, or starting a new enterprise, for he is regarded as the deity of luck.

Right: Inside this elaborately carved window on the second floor of a Kathmandu house, is an awesome mask representing Bhairav, the god of terror, guardian deity of Indra Chowk.

"dressed" in new robes and garlanded with flowers and jewelled necklets.

More devotees throng to Pashupatinath for the annual Shiva Ratri, a night consecrated to Shiva. Thousands of pilgrims from all over Nepal and India attend. Some fly or drive, but many walk the entire distance, for the more one suffers on the journey the more merit one attains. They camp in the sacred woods around the temple where in remote times Shiva dwelt, disguised as a deer. Naked sadhus, saffron-robed yogis and ascetics, city women in silk saris, village girls in homespun, farmers and businessmen, rich and poor alike congregate to pay homage to the Great God.

Downstream are the burning ghats for cremating

Left: Pigeons swoop to pick up rice offerings left by devotees in the courtyard of the Setho Machhendrenath Temple, in the heart of old Kathmandu.

Right: Kneeling outside the temple, a pious devotee uses a taper to light traditional Nepalese lamps, twisted cotton wicks in small clay bowls of mustard oil. When used for *puja*, or worship, the lamps must always number 108, an auspicious number in Hindu symbolism.

Regimental standards flutter over piles of decapitated buffalo and goat's heads, victims of the army's annual sacrifice for the Dasain festival. Gurkha soldiers armed with curved knives must lop off the heads of the animals in one swoop. Then the headless beast is dragged about the banners, smearing the ground with blood, and thus ensuring a successful year ahead. This rite is performed in the Kot Courtyard, opposite the old Hanuman Dhoka palace, site of a bloody coup in the mid-19th century which ousted the Shah rulers and began the century-long Rana rule.

the dead, whose ashes float into the holy Ganges releasing their souls to heaven. One circular cement platform stands apart from the others. This is the royal burning ghat. When King Tribhuvan died in a Swiss clinic in 1955, his body was flown home and then borne through crowds of weeping mourners with shaved heads, who for thirteen days had slept on straw, ate no salt and taken just one meal a day. At the sandalwood funeral pyre, a Brahmin priest sliced a piece of flesh from the king's midriff to be buried on a sacred island in the Bagmati, and cut a piece of bone from his forehead to be placed in another sacred river. Yet another piece of bone was used to contaminate the priest's food, for he had taken upon himself all the late king's sins thus freeing Tribhuvan's

Left: Fingering his *mani* beads, a Buddhist rosary, a Tibetan monk circumambulates the base of the 2,000-year-old stupa at Swayambhunath. Behind him, are a row of copper prayer wheels embossed with the Tibetan mantra *Om Mani Padme Hum.* Buddhists believe that by spinning the metal drums they are symbolically turning the wheel of the law — the cycle of life and death.

Right: Surrounding Bodhnath are Tibetan monasteries, known as *gompas*, where young boys are admitted as monks and schooled in the Buddhist way of life. Devotees believe that by following this path, known as the *dharma*, one can escape the endless cycle of rebirths and achieve nirvana, or self-enlightenment.

soul for eternal bliss. By shouldering this burden, the now sin-laden priest lost his Brahmin caste and was forever exiled to India. His worker's compensation however, amounted to 10,000 rupees in alms, two elephants and other gifts to the tune of 200,000 rupees which must have considerably softened the blow of having to descend the caste ladder.

Nepal may be a Hindu kingdom, but the one symbol that dominates the Kathmandu Valley more than any other is Buddhist. These are the mysterious, enigmatic "all-seeing eyes" painted on the tops of the great stupas, on temple doors, on the wheels of the festival chariots and even adorning Kathmandu tourist T-shirts. With their awesome Mongolian gaze narrowed by drooping lids, they seem to penetrate the valley with unceasing vigilance. Under the eyes is a question-mark nose (actually the Nepalese symbol of "one") and between them is a snail-like symbol which is the

Buddha's third eye.

Nowhere are the eyes as powerful as at Swayambhunath, the great 2,000-year-old hilltop stupa overlooking the city. I had strong memories of this, the valley's holiest Buddhist shrine, for it was here that I first made my acquaintance with those indomitable Buddhists, the Tibetans. In those days there was a sward of grass at the base of the hill and refugee Tibetans who had made the arduous mountain journey from their Chinese-conquered homeland were camped there. They were a sight to behold, for then Tibet was even more mysterious and remote than Nepal. Few had cut their long braids, entwined with red wool and roped about their heads. Men and women alike sported this unique

unisex hairstyle. They wore long Mongolian-style robes, brocaded hats lined with fur, and yak-skin boots trimmed with embroidered felt.

Two decades later, like a phantom from the past, a Tibetan woman in her long *chuba* dress and braided hair is chanting and prostrating herself at the bottom of the 300 steps that lead to the famed stupa. Monkeys still rule the wooded hill, sliding down the iron banisters with babies clinging to their backs and swooping on any unsuspecting visitor who is foolish enough to snack in their presence. The beggar children and the ganja and curio sellers are still there, bobbing up from among the stone *chaityas* that line the path. But every other reminiscence pales when I climb the final step. There atop the massive white dome, accosting me, are those enigmatic "all-seeing eyes". Under their watchful gaze dozens of cooing pigeons preen themselves under strings of prayer flags that flutter like washing on a line. At the various gilded shrines around the base, monkeys

In Hindu mythology each god or goddess has its own carrier. This gleaming bronze rat, known as Muso, is the vehicle for Ganesh, the elephant-headed god. It is often seen guarding his master's shrines.

stealthily insert their arms through metal grilles and make off with the devotees' delicacies, food for the gods. But then Swayambhunath's monkeys are also sacred. Tibetans and Nepalese alike circumambulate the great hemisphere, twirling brass prayer wheels engraved with the sacred mantra, *Om Mani Padme Hum* — "Hail to the Jewel in the Heart of the Lotus".

Bodhnath, the valley's other great Buddhist stupa, is even larger than Swayambhunath, but is only considered holy by Tibetan Buddhists, not the Nepalese. Above another pair of strangely arresting eyes is a gilded "steeple" which ascends the thirteen steps to the Buddhist heaven. Once Bodhnath arose dramatically from the farmlands, but today

Milk flows down the body of Nandi — a stone bull who is Shiva's servant and companion — at the Vajra Varahi Temple in a sacred grove of trees near Chapagaon. The dog riding the stone beast makes a tasty snack of the devotee's offerings.

it is flanked by an ever-increasing tide of Tibetan monasteries, houses and carpet factories. This is now the centre of Tibetan society in Nepal. Yet pilgrims have been making the arduous journey from beyond the Himalayas for centuries, long before the Tibetans fled from the communists. One hundred years ago, a historian remarked that "Bodhnath is without contradiction the headquarters of human putrefaction." He went on to say that the Tibetans were dressed in "filthy tatters with oily skins that have never soiled water." He wouldn't recognise the place today. The stupa is much the same, but Tibetan traders now dress in imported clothes, make their circumambulations in Adidas running shoes and pull out Japanese calculators to convert rupees to dollars. A banner flutters above a curio shop proclaiming "For World Peace use Pancha Buddha Tibetan Incense."

For centuries, before the Tibetans flocked to Bodhnath, Patan was the thriving hub of Buddhist scholarship and art. Many of the *bahals* (former monastic

A bronze, flower-bedecked deity as viewed through a perforated metal screen at the Temple of the White Machhendrenath in Kathmandu. This idol, a gift from a rich patron, is one of dozens which crowd the temple precinct. The main deity, the Seto (White) Machhendrenath, is installed in the centre of the temple in a sacred shrine. It is paraded annually through the streets in a festive chariot processsion and is identified as a manifestation of the Buddhist saint, Avolokithwara.

compounds) which exist today are proof of the glorious past of Newar Buddhism. But they lost their colonies of celibate monks long ago when a zealous orthodox Brahmin conquered the valley, destroyed 84,000 manuscripts and forced the monks to marry. Much later, under the tolerant Hindu Malla kings, Buddhism thrived again, but after the Gurkha conquest, temples and monasteries were left to their own resources and another era of poverty ensued.

But as a writer once remarked, "the religions pass away and the festivals remain." Nowhere is this more true than in Kathmandu Valley where the Newars not only celebrate the great Hindu and Buddhist events, but have their own folkloric festivals known as *jatras*, when images of gods are drawn in *raths*, chariots with ponderous wooden wheels that are up to twelve metres long. Bhaktapur has its thrilling

Bisket festival at Nepalese New Year, when the awesome Bhairav and his female counterpart, Goddess Bhadrakali, are pulled through the streets in towering temple-shaped *raths*. Kathmandu has its Indrajatra, when the girl-child Kumari, the Living Goddess, is borne through the city's streets. And Patan hosts possibly the most famous and most spectacular of all - the Rato Machhendrenath Rath Jatra — the chariot procession of the Red Machhendrenath.

Bungamati was built at an auspicious site and is home for the Machhendrenath for several months of the year. His image — a red wooden slab with painted eyes — is carried from Bungamati to Patan for the magnificent annual chariot procession. Hundreds of devotees swarm to touch the sacred chariot and those who pull the ropes are considered especially fortunate. Above this mobile throne room is a fifteen-metre-high steeple, bedecked with pine branches and garlands, which sways perilously close to the buildings of Patan on the ponderous chariot journey. The great lumbering vehicle only progresses a few city blocks each day and it may not reach its destination at Jawalkhel, on the far side of Patan, until months later. Astrologers calculate its every movement and if something inauspicious happens — a wheel falling off, or like in 1969 when the chariot caught fire — the people are uneasy. This bodes ill for the coming year and perhaps the life-giving rains will fail to come.

An unquestioning belief in their gods pervades the Kathmandu Valley, where a melange of faiths mingle and co-exist with a tolerance seldom seen elsewhere on this planet. It explains why the Indian and Buddhist sages, who trekked here in bygone times, referred to the valley as the "Himalayan Paradise."

Among the thousands of shrines in the Kathmandu Valley, very few are neglected, particularly at festival times when every deity — whether carved in brass on a temple door, sculpted in stone or even sunk into the pavements — is smeared with sacred powders and garlanded with marigolds, barley shoots and even buffalo intestines.

Above: From the tops of Buddhist stupas, these strangely arresting eyes peer out at worshippers. Between them is a mystic third eye, symbolizing true wisdom. The odd "question-mark" nose is actually the number *ek*, or one, in the Nepali language, a symbol of unity.

Left: On the last day of the Dasain festival, every Hindu worshipper is adorned with a *tikka* of vermilion powder, rice and milk curd, pressed to their foreheads as a blessing of good fortune.

CHAPTER 8

Architectural Traditions

"Cresting a low range of hills, which runs along the valley, we at length came in sight of Kathmandoo. This is another most remarkable view, and a very beautiful one. A picturesque quaint-looking temple, and a cluster of red wide-eaved houses, profusely adorned with carved wood work, form a pretty foreground; in the plain below is a broad river, on the opposite bank of which stands the town, with its numberless Chinese-looking temples, the brasswork with which they are ornamented glittering in the sun."

This extract from Francis Egerton's *Journal of a Winter's Tour in India: With a Visit to the Court of Nepaul* was written in 1852. Apart from the mushrooming of cement buildings, the bane of architectural aesthetes, and the anomaly of a large hunk of land shaved from the valley's farmlands — where jumbo jets land with surprising regularity — most of the valley still looks as Egerton found it.

Travellers, writers and romantics have long enthused over the setting of the Vale of Kathmandu, yet other places also have stunning backdrops. There are Kashmir and Ladakh and even Hunza in Pakistan, but none have anything like the outstanding traditional architecture that characterizes the Kathmandu Valley. Only here are found the gilded, tiered pagoda temples, the wood and brick palaces with their spacious squares, the four-storey townhouses that cluster in compact villages and cities; all adorned and ornamented with beaten brass and wood carvings as intricate as lace.

The gifted Newars created this superb architecture. Where this race of talented artisans originated is still a much disputed question for Asian anthropologists. But there is an even bigger puzzle, and one that has inspired many a scholarly architectural thesis. Is Nepal the birthplace of

Patan's Durbar Square has long been famed as hosting the most splendid collection of buildings in Nepal. The royal palace and its courtyards are to the east, and in the west are at least a dozen temples of different architectural styles. It's no wonder Patan was sometimes known as "the city of a thousand golden roofs."

115

the pagoda? Some scholars assert the pagoda came from India to Nepal, then onwards through Tibet into China and lastly to Japan. They quote as evidence the accounts of seventh-century Chinese pilgrims who describe "squares crowded with multi-storied monasteries and golden-topped temples" in Kathmandu. Other historians discount the India origin on the grounds that Nepal's shrines have little in common with the South Indian shikhara temples to which the Portuguese apparently first applied the name pagoda. Chinese pagodas definitely look more like the Nepalese version, yet their silhouette is not as dynamic, as the roofs don't diminish in size as much. The closest ally would seem to be the loftier but less substantial Meru pagoda monuments of Bali. Both have been called "earthbound arrows pointing to the sky." The fact remains that these unique pagodas, found throughout Nepal in such magnificent abundance, may have borrowed some aspects from foreign cultures, but they remain uniquely Nepalese.

The most intriguing pagoda theory, and the one that seems the most likely in view of the valley's geographical setting, is that they derive from the pyramid shape of the great Himalayan peaks. This theory has long been espoused by local religious leaders, but was first put to paper by E.B. Havell in his book *The Ancient and Medieval Architecture of India*. Amongst the many great peaks named after the gods and godesses — like Nanda Devi, Annapurna and Ganesh Himal — the holiest is the 6,700-metre Kailasa (Kailash) in Tibet, home of Shiva and the dominant peak in Hinduism's sacred landscape. This awesome mountain, with its near vertical faces of golden-coloured limestone, is considered a giant, natural temple. Pilgrims venture to this remote frozen place to circumambulate and prostrate around the pyramidal peak, which bears an uncanny resemblance to a Nepalese pagoda.

In Nepal, religion governs art. So it's not that far-fetched to see the inspiration of the pagoda deriving from the great Abode of the Gods, which not only dominates religion, but the landscape as well. There is another fascinating link between religion, art and architecture — the *mandala*. This is a sacred diagram which shows the way through the tangle of universal conflicting forces to the "Oneness of the Absolute." In nature, according to the sacred Hindu texts, Lake Manasasarovana, at the foot of Mount Kailasa, is the mandala to this soaring natural temple. It follows that as the mandala is a map of the universe and also a geometric projection of the world, brought further into focus, it serves as a plan for any temple. The three-dimensional building arises from the two-dimensional plan with the mandala as blueprint. The square shape, representing the "sacred palace" of the mandala, corresponds to the plinth at the base of the pagoda. Enclosed in this are multiple circles that serve as protection and demarcate the sacred area about the shrine.

In a land where religion is the dominant force, architects, sculptors, carpenters and bronzeworkers all labour under the guiding light of priests, and to directions laid down in ancient texts first revealed by Bishwakarma. In the Mahabharata he is called the "Master of a Thousand Handicrafts, carpenter of the gods and builder of their places divine, fashioner of every jewel, first of craftsmen, by whose art men live, and whom, a great and deathless god they continually worship." Bishwakarma remains the patron diety and inspiration of all Nepalese craftsmen, whose egoless endeavours are as much directed to pleasing their gods as their patrons.

These same principles also apply to local domestic

A detail of Newari wood-carving above and on the right, Bhaktapur's ochre-coloured brick buildings take on a mellow glow in the late afternoon. Rearing above Taumadi Tole is Nepal's tallest pagoda, the five-tiered Nyatapola Temple, and at right angles to it is the Kasi Bishwanath Temple which was rebuilt after the destructive 1934 earthquake.

architecture. All palaces, monasteries and townhouses are basically brick and wood structures following the same building methods. As a result, Newar cities and towns with their ruddy brick and ochre hues, their red-tiled roofs and dark decorative woodwork, present a most aesthetic and harmonious appearance. Until recently, most growth in Newar towns was vertical. They went up instead of out in order to preserve the valley's valuable farming land.

Traditional houses have thick walls of three or four storeys, built around a courtyard connected to the street by a tunnel-like entrance. As the Newars are great traders, part of the ground floor is often open to the street as a shop or work area with a facade of elaborately carved wooden columns.

Wood carving in Nepal is more an art than a craft, as evidenced by these skilfully decorated house facades in Kathmandu. The Newari language has a rich vocabulary of wood carving terms and the precise techniques for executing this decorative work, which uses no nails or glue, are still preserved in medieval texts, passed down through generations of craftsmen.

Behind these, around the courtyard, are cattle stalls and storerooms. Up a dark narrow flight of stairs on the second level is the *nal*, the main living and sleeping room, where light streams in through the profusely carved windows which often run the entire length of the house. The third level, also well lit and ventilated, is where guests are entertained and much of the family activity takes place. This is as far as many guests can penetrate, for the top floor, given over to the kitchen and shrine room, is off limits to "the impure" — not just non-Hindus, but also those of a low-caste and even those who are not members of the immediate family. Cooking and the handling of food is dictated by the same rules which determine where each caste, according to occupation, lives in a neighbourhood. This system has become slightly eroded in Kathmandu, but in more traditional towns like Bhaktapur it still exists. As you wander the streets it becomes apparent that goldsmiths, who are often priests as well, live in the highest section of town. Potters, slightly down the caste-scale, congregate in the mid-section, while the low-caste butchers and tailors live at the base of the hill. So yet again this pattern of vertical heirachy repeats itself through the floors of a house and through the levels of town — yet another image of the mandala in three-dimensional form.

Just as the birth of a child is a most propitious event, so also is the birth of a house, which involves much the same rituals as in the erection of temples. At the selected site, a goat is sacrificed to pacify spirits who dwell in the ground — a necessary precaution in the Kathmandu Valley where earthquakes are as frequent as they are destructive. On the next auspicious day, calculated by an astrologer/priest, the foundation stone is laid and offerings of cloth, ducks' eggs, a

coconut and betel nuts are made. The *dakarmi*, the chief house builder, places five brass vessels and a silver tortoise into the foundations and covers them with bricks. The spirits are now appeased and the construction can begin. As each floor is completed, different *pujas* are enacted, more goats are sacrificed, and then at the *thaima puja*, a family feast held when the roof is completed, the house is considered to be born.

Some buildings are obviously more favoured by the gods than others. The five-storey Nyatapola temple in Bhaktapur stood firm even through the awesome quake of 1934, when seventy percent of the town's buildings were destroyed or damaged. Legend has it that at the foundation ceremony, a Jyapu, a man of the farming caste, sowed some rice. Later, when he went to pull out the plants, he needed a spade to dig them up. This folktale is quoted to show the stability of the temple's foundations. It is proof too of the soundness of Newar brick building, one of the oldest industries in the valley. According to ancient Buddhist annals, brick and tile making were thriving crafts 20,000 years ago when Manjushree, the drainer of the lake that was Kathmandu Valley, built his first city — from bricks, of course. More tangible evidence of the trade's antiquity came to life recently with the discovery of a brick impressed with characters that link it to the ancient city of King Amsuvarman, 1,300 years

The pinnacle is the topmost point of a temple and symbolically is one of its most important features. Pinnacles can be cone-shaped, metal spires or gilded umbrellas. But at Bagh Bhairav Temple in Kirtipur, a dozen golden spires are arrayed along the roof, the centre one protected with an unusual metal canopy. These same pinnacles are repeated on the lower roofs as well, for the temple builders thought that multiples of such an auspicious symbol would only enhance the sacredness of the site.

ago. As with many art forms, the oldest specimens are often the finest and some of the valley's earliest terracotta wares were of exceptional quality. As with bricks made in ancient Rome and Egypt, the old Nepalese bricks are also much larger than those produced today. But the techniques are little changed. Bricks are still hand-moulded and fired on the site using traditional wood-fueled kilns. Roofing and paving tiles are made in a similar manner, but they are coated with a special clay, high in iron oxide, which gives them their characteristic deep red colour.

From a distance, bricks and tiles colour the cityscape. Yet on closer inspection, it's the intricate woodwork that gives Nepalese architecture its unique appearance. Across

Guardian lions flank the entrance to the hilltop temple of Changu Narayan, twelve kilometres east of Kathmandu. This pagoda is the oldest Vishnu temple in Nepal, dating back to the fourth century, and also a repository of priceless stone sculptures including the most archaic inscription so far discovered in the valley.

balconies, around doors and window frames, sculptured into roof struts, engraved on columns, lintels and cornices — on every exposed wooden surface — is evidence of the heights attained by the Newar carpenters. One 19th-century author raves: "the truculent fancy of a joyous imagination has carved out peacocks, nymphs, nagas, elephants, flowers, leaves and erotic monstrosities."

This inspired handiwork is not limited to temples, but often reaches its greatest artistic heights on domestic buildings, especially in the rows of ornamented windows. Personal expression runs rampant in window decoration. They can be square, rectangular, arched, oval or round; they are open, shuttered or screened with wood carved in squares, sunbursts, stars, diamonds, interwoven snakes or the feathers of a peacock's tail. Often, on a ledge below is a frieze of Surya, the sun god, flanked by teams of galloping horses. And a window never has vermilion powder sprinkled upon it, for this is not a shrine, merely a showpiece for the woodcarver's craft — a symbol of his artistic inventiveness.

The torana, a hemispherical crest above temple doors, is another venue of powerful woodcarving expression, but decoration here is much more iconographic and always follows a set religious pattern. Usually found in the middle is an image of the deity who is enshrined at the temple. Above this is Garuda, the birdman, grappling with snakes and exhaling clouds of breath that make up the border of the torana. Underneath are *makaras*, mythical crocodiles. The most graceful and finest work is often found on the temple roof struts, carved representations of the guardian deities, the attendants of the major god depicted on the torana. Although the struts are flat at the back, they give the appearance of being carved in the round, and as they tilt out to support the temple roof, they are easily viewed. The base of the strut usually depicts erotica, bizarre hell scenes or landscapes — but of much inferior craftsmanship to the central god who is always the dominant character. They can be ferocious or gentle, two-armed or multi-armed like a sunburst. Sometimes they are angelic females known as *apsaras*, or forest dryads called *yaksis*, and among these are the most graceful, seductive and oldest wood sculptures of the valley. Unlike windows, the struts are often garishly painted. This tends to offend Western aesthetic sensibilities, but it's an essential part of their religious significance.

Temples are also lavishly ornamented with patron's gifts. These can be princely donations: gleaming gilded roofs, canopies and pinnacles; hundreds of brass bells which hang from the eaves and tinkle in the faintest breeze. There are stone columns topped with life-size brass figures of medieval Malla kings. There are doors and toranas of hammered brass repousse work and great gilt belts that dangle from the uppermost roofs. And there are the bronze idols, an art that Newar craftsmen perfected centuries ago. Their medieval method — the *cire perdue* or lost wax technique — is still used today, and the ancestors of these artisans are credited with introducing this technique of bronze casting into Tibet. Much older than the bronzes though, are the stone sculptures of the valley, many of which date back to Licchavi times, the fourth to ninth century AD. Among the earliest masterpieces are the Vishnu sculptures at Changu Narayan. But the oldest Vishnu sculpture, dated to 467 AD, stands in the National Museum. It depicts the legend of Vishnu as Vamana the dwarf, reclaiming the earth from the demons. The most famous of all the valley's ancient stone art works is the ninth-century Maya Deva, showing the Buddha's nativity. This polished, black stone relief, also in the National Museum, shows Maya Deva, Buddha's mother, gracefully posed under the mango tree where she felt her first birth pangs. A sturdy baby Buddha stands next to her on a lotus petal while two angels pour water on him from lotus buds. Stone sculpture attained its highest form in these early days when the challenge was in inventing the deities forms. In later years rigidity set in when sculptures had to conform to iconographic rules. These works lack the vitality and grace of the earlier masterpieces.

Over the centuries many of the valley's buildings and temples have undergone dozens of restorations, or been destroyed by earthquakes and then painstakingly rebuilt brick by brick. If this had happened elsewhere, the old buildings would have been razed and a modern structure would have taken its place. But in the Kathmandu Valley, where materials and construction methods differ little from those used centuries ago, this isn't the case. The biggest

Rows of columns grace the ground floor of the 17th-century Bishwanath Mandir Temple in Patan. Bridging the columns are a series of carved crests, known as *toranas*, which depict the deity in the centre surrounded by mythical crocodiles and topped by a *garuda*, the flying "birdman."

124

threats to tradition, as in most third world countries, are ugly cement block buildings. They have cancerously encroached on the new suburban parts of Kathmandu and even filtered into Patan. Residents complain they aren't as warm as the conventional homes, and in these cold damp interiors the people have developed rheumatic illnesses never known in the valley before. Aesthetically, they stand out like the proverbial sore thumb among the earthy tones of traditional architecture. Yet Bhaktapur maintains its aesthetic wholeness, as do most of the other smaller Newar towns.

One day I found myself in Bungamati, the home of the Newar deity the Red Machhendrenath, and a village once under the orbit of the Kingdom of Patan. Here is a town that

Multi-armed guardian deities adorn the roof struts of Kathmandu's temples as the culminating glory of the woodcarvers' talents. Unlike the unpainted carvings on doors and windows, these are brightly coloured — part of the spritual symbolism .

Far right: At the base of the strut are erotic carvings which, although crudely carved, number among the most famous, or infamous, carvings in the valley.

is absolutely timeless. The terracotta houses have overhanging eaves that almost touch above the narrow cobblestoned alleys, where women sit carding and spinning wool, and where men hew logs into planks with antiquated cross-cut saws. In the town square, girls pull buckets from a well, crops dry in the sun, and corn and garlic hang in garlands from the heavy wooden windows. Only one house has glass — in some of its windows — and there were no signs, no cold drink shops, no cement houses, no metal roofs and surprisingly, not even a motorbike to spoil the medieval aura. This is the most time-warped place I have ever visited. Months later I was surprised to learn that Bungamati was razed by the 1934 earthquake. It was incredible to think that this architecturally homogenous town had been rebuilt since then. Proof of the enduring skills of the Newar craftsmen, the creators of Kathmandu's unique architecture.

Annapurna: Mother Earth, goddess of plenty, whose abode is the Annapurna range near Pokhara.

apsaras: Angelic female figures carved into wooden struts supporting the upper roofs of pagodas.

asana: Symbolic sitting postures of the gods; also a throne or pedestal on which the icon is sitting.

Ashta Matrikas: Eight mother goddesses who represent the female personas of male Hindu deities.

ayudhas: Traditional attributes or weapons which accompany the gods, ie the conch shell of Vishnu or trident of Shiva.

bahal: Newar Buddhist monastery enclosing a courtyard.

bhanga: Prescribed iconographic body postures of the deities.

bodhisattva: Person who has achieved Buddhahood, but who chooses to remain on earth to teach in order to enlighten others.

Bhairav: Shiva as the god of terror.

Bhimsen: Deified war hero and strongman who became patron saint of merchants.

Brahma: The Great Creator who formed the world and everything in it, including the caste system. Brahmin priests issued from his head, warriors from his arms, merchants and landowners from his legs, labourers from his feet.

Brahmin: Highest Hindu caste, originally priests.

chaityas: Smaller version of the Buddhist, bell-shaped stupa. Sometimes contains holy scriptures.

Dasain: Joyous harvest festival to appease Durga, when thousands of animals are sacrificed.

dharmasala: Resthouse for the use of pilgrims and travellers, adjoining temples and monasteries.

Durga: Awesome form of Shiva's consort; animals are sacrificed at her shrines.

Garuda: Mythical creature, half-human and half-eagle, the traditional vehicle of Vishnu; often appears on crests above temple doors.

Gautama Buddha: Founder of Buddhism, born in Lumbini, Nepal in the sixth century BC.

Ganesh: Elephant-headed god of wisdom and success, the defender and remover of obstacles; is propitiated first before the worship of other gods.

Ganga: Deity representing India's holiest river, the Ganges; often guards shrine entrances together with her "sister" Jamuna and always stands on a mythical sea monster (*makara*).

ganja: Dried flowering tips of the marijuana plant; favourite herb of Lord Shiva.

ghat: Stepped platforms on riverbanks for bathing and cremation.

gompa: Monastery of Tibetan or Lama Buddhism.

Gorakhnath: Popular incarnation of Shiva; historically a yogi who founded a Shaivite cult in the 11th century.

Green Tara (Harita Tara): Historically a Nepalese princess, now deified by Buddhists and Hindus alike.

Hanuman: Deified monkey and hero of the epic Ramayana.

Holi: Ancient Hindu festival when coloured powder is thrown about with wild abandon.

Indrajatra: Eight-day festival in September to honour Indra, the King of Gods.

Jamuna: Goddess of purity and devotion, who together with Ganga guards entrances to shrines; she always stands on a tortoise (*kurma*).

Janai Purnima: Annual festival when Brahmin's body strings are renewed for the coming year.

jatra: Traditional Newar processions when a decorated idol is carried about in a chariot.

khadga: Symbolic sword of enlightenment, used to destroy ignorance; special symbol of Manjushree and shaped like the original town plan of Kathmandu.

Krishna: Vishnu's eighth and most beloved incarnation; the ideal of manhood and a promise of ultimate triumph of good over evil in the hearts of men.

kumari: Young virgin regarded as a living goddess in Kathmandu Valley towns; she is a representation of Taleju, the Royal Goddess.

Lakshmi: Senior wife of Vishnu; the goddess of wealth and beauty.

lingam: Phallic symbol of Shiva.

Machhendrenath: Guardian god of the Kathmandu Valley, and guarantor of rain for rice-planting; popular interpretation of Avolokithwara, the Buddhist god of mercy.

makaras: Mythical crocodile or sea monster often depicted on woodcarvings over temple entrances.

mandala: Literally means a "circle"; a sacred tantric diagram used as a visual aid in meditation.

Manjushree: Legendary patriarch of Kathmandu Valley who drained the waters of the former lake.

mantra: Sacred Buddhist syllables chanted during meditation.

mudra: Symbolic hand gestures; ie *Namaskara*, when hands are brought together in prayer which became the Nepalese greeting *namaste*.

naga: Serpents worshipped as divine beings, a remnant of early fertility rites.

Naga Panchami: Annual day for worship of snake gods who bring rain, grant increased wealth and protect the family treasures.

Narayan: Local name for Vishnu, the second god of the Hindu trinity.

Pashupathi: Shiva as Lord of the Animals, symbolized by the lingam.

pata: Ancient Sanskrit religious scroll.

paubha: Traditional Newar religious painting similar to a Tibetan thangka.

puja: Ritual offerings and prayers to the gods.

Rahu: Mysterious, malevolent planet in Hindu astrology.

Glossary of the Gods

rath: Wooden chariots with large wheels used to carry deities in processions.

sadhu: Wandering holy man; generally Shaivites, followers of Shiva.

saligram: Smooth, fossilized stone sacred to Vishnu and found only in Kali Ghandaki Gorge.

serthang: Religious cloth painting with a gold background.

shikhara: Stone or brick temple with a tall central spire.

Shiva: Third in the Hindu triad and the most awesome of gods; the Creator and Destroyer, the force of procreation and the god of reproduction.

stupa: Large, bell-shaped Buddhist relic chamber.

suttee: Former practice of Hindu widows, who threw themselves on their husband's funeral pyres.

Taleju: Chief protectress of the Kathmandu Valley and a mild incarnation of Durga; it's believed the king draws his power from her; Kumari, the living goddess, is her representative.

tala pattra: Ancient Sanskrit books painted on palm leaves.

Tantric: Secretive occult form of Hinduism (Shaktism) and Buddhism (Vajrayana) which advocates the use of all means, including sex, to attain enlightenment within one life span.

thangka: Religious scroll-painting originally used for meditation purposes.

tikka: Red powder spot applied to the forehead between the eyes; symbolizes the presence of the divine.

torana: Decorative, hemispherical crest suspended over the entrance to a shrine.

Vishnu: Second in the Hindu trinity, he is the Preserver and Protector of all that Brahma created.

yaksis: Mythical forest dryads often carved into the roof struts of pagodas.

CHAPTER 9

Art as Worship

An 18th-century *thangka*, a tantric religious painting done on cloth, depicts Bhairav, a powerful deity who represents the awesome, destructive force of Shiva. He is shown in sexual union with his female consort. This anonymous painting, at the National Art Gallery in Bhaktapur, measures 82 x 64 centimetres.

ven Picasso was old hat when the Renaissance finally caught up in Nepal. Until the 20th century, Nepalese art was essentially religious and symbolic. Religion and art was inseparable, the idea of art for art's sake had yet to arrive in the sequestered kingdom of Kathmandu. Art was confined to banner painting, manuscript illustrations, royal murals and *thangkas* for meditation. The object of art was worship and devotion; the image was a means to realising a higher consciousness, not a representation of reality. Every motif and figure — even the design, shape, size and colour — was done to strictly religious guidelines laid down centuries ago. There was no room for personal expression: the skill was faithful reproduction. Artists practised their trade in the anonymity of caste, and no artwork bore its creator's signature for they were traditionally without fame as individuals. His reward was in the sacred rites of artistic creation, for he transformed himself as well as his materials.

Artists were like any other craftsman, unlike the Western world's conception of the painter as being in the more esoteric 'fine arts' which were considered to be on a higher plane than mere crafts. European art history is full of artists who broke with family traditions to take up the risky business of art. Thin, emaciated artists starving in garrets, were a popular image of how one would fare if fated to follow the arts as a career. Not so in Nepal, for there was no choice, one simply followed the trade of one's forefathers. Occupations were hereditary and strictly according to caste. No craftsmen could encroach upon the professional rights of others, except in the unique case of the Nalli, who were allowed to supplement their earnings, as their sole artistic

occupation was to paint the eye of an image at certain religious festivals. Chitrakara, was the artist caste, and even today some artists still use this name.

Painting was probably introduced from India during the Licchavi period, the fourth to ninth century AD, in the form of Sanskrit palm-leaf books, known as *tala pattra*, colourfully illustrated in the style of medieval European illuminated manuscripts. Often the wooden boards which served as covers were lacquered and painted with religious deities, particularly "the ten incarnations of Vishnu", a favourite theme of the Licchavis. Paper superseded palm leaves, reaching India in the 12th century and then filtered into Nepal.

Fresco painting arrived in India before the fifth century AD, and could have reached Nepal not long after. No example remains from these early eras and even the fragments of medieval palace and temple frescoes that survive today, give merely a glimpse into an art form once utilized as the major wall decoration of Kathmandu's ruling class.

One day, as I strolled through the National Art Gallery, formerly the Bhaktapur Royal Palace, I found myself in a most unusual room which overlooked Durbar Square. Frescoes, reminiscent of Rajasthan, covered the walls and window niches. Pieces were missing, and much was indistinct, but I could still pick out palace scenes, floral friezes, gods on clouds and a large central *mandala*, in deep shades of terracotta red, white and black. This gallery is unknown in the guidebooks. No-one knew much about it at all, for it appears that until recently the frescoes were obscured by an opaque film of soot, dust and oil. They were rediscovered after responding to a chemical treatment, bringing to light an almost forgotten form of Nepalese art.

Right: Sacred palm leaf books were probably the first painted medium to reach Nepal. This well-preserved example, called a *pancha raksha*, is written in Sanskrit with small paintings of gods in the middle of each leaf, or page. It is dated 1247 AD and is in the National Art Gallery at Bhaktapur.

Far right: This finely painted 11th-century wooden cover for a palm-leaf book depicts the ten incarnations of Vishnu, including that of Buddha. In the National Art Gallery, Bhaktapur, it measures 10 x 51 centimetres.

Thangka painting apparently arrived in Nepal from northern India as Buddhist refugees fled the conquering Moslem hordes. Its scroll-like form probably derived from China, as these sacred images had to be portable for travelling monks who used them as teaching and meditation aids.

One thousand years later, the thangka painters of Kathmandu still use basically the same techniques. In a small room, lit only by natural light which streams through the old

carved windows, I watch as a young apprentice stretches a thangka onto a wooden frame and prepares the unbleached cotton cloth with a liquid paste of lime, glue and flour. After it dries, he will rub it with a smooth stone, or as his ancestors would have preferred, a conch shell. Karma Lama, the guru of the atelier, who's been painting thangkas for twenty years, sketches the main deity with India ink. In former times, he would have used charcoal or lamp black. The patterns are stored in his head, but he still works according to iconographic rules passed down through the ages. Rules inspired by Tantra, the esoteric mystic religious cult, written in a deliberately obscure fashion to keep the doctrines secret from the unitiated. Every iconographic sign prescribed in the Tantric scriptures carries a hidden meaning and only the initiated know the key. Karma Lama knows the appropriate *mudras*

(hand gestures), *asanas* (sitting positions), *bhangas* (body postures) *ayudhas* (attributes) ornaments and colours of each diety, and before the creation of each thangka he visualizes that particular god or goddess so the image will be a more effective tool for meditation. Karma Lama still uses what he terms "stone colours" — the natural mineral and organic paints of his forefathers. But many ateliers that turn out cheap thangkas for the tourist trade use aniline paints introduced in the 19th century. In the old days, Nepalese paints were considered far superior to Tibetan varieties, and when a painter travelled to Lhasa he carried his own ground lapis lazuli for blue, arsenic for yellow, and gold dust for making the famed *serthang*, a scroll with a golden background.

Until the middle of the 17th century, Nepalese styles dominated thangka painting, but the trend reversed and Tibetan artists influenced by Tantric's sexual mysticism invented a new range of Tibetan demonology, replacing the benign and benevolent Nepalese Buddhas and Bodhisattvas. The extent of Tibetan influence is evident in the name "thangka" which is the Tibetan term for what was originally called a *paubha* in Nepal. Nowadays, one finds few old thangkas or paubhas in good shape. Frequent rolling cracks the paint, humidity takes its toll, and many are stained by the soot from monastery butter lamps, a trick some unscrupulous dealers use to produce "antique" thangkas. Of course, many of the nation's greatest art works have found their way into foreign collections, the plight of poor countries the world over. However, some old paubhas still exist, coveted as sacred religious relics in the Buddhist monasteries of Patan and Kathmandu. Once a year, during Gunla, the sacred month of Lord Buddha, these ancient relics are put on public view. Thousands of devotees come to see the ancient illumi-

134

Above: A colourful mural in the "naive landscape" style by an anonymous local painter. It shows all the major temples, Durbar Squares and palaces of the Kathmandu Valley. The mural adorns the walls of the Yak and Yeti Hotel in Kathmandu.

nated manuscripts, precious idols, antique paubhas and the even rarer *patas*, Buddhist epics painted horizontally on cloth in comic-strip fashion. Many of these treasures date from the valley's artistic zenith in the 15th and 16th centuries, a peaceful and prosperous era when Nepalese art flourished under the patronage of the Malla kings. After 1768, when Gurkha King Prithvi Narayan Shah conquered the valley, the arts degenerated. Unlike the Mallas, the Gurkhas were more interested in nation building and military escapades than supporting culture. In 1846, after the bloody Kot Massacre, the Rana prime ministers took control of Nepal and the Shah kings were reduced to mere puppet figures. This was another turning point for the arts, as the Rana nobility initiated travel to Europe and for the first time Western ideas filtered back to the medieval art scene of Kathmandu.

Half a millenium after Europe's artistic rebirth, the Renaissance finally came to Kathmandu. Local artisans discovered there was more to art than the faithful reproductions of thangkas and paubhas, that art was more than a vehicle for religious devotions. They discovered new techniques and mediums; oils and watercolours took over from gouache; scrolls and walls were superseded by imported canvas and drawing paper; three-dimensional realism suddenly inspired an art scene schooled in the two-dimensional Eastern tradition. And most significant of all, Nepal's artists found their egos.

From this turbulent cultural era, two painters emerged as leaders of the new movement. Chandra Man Singh Maskey and Tej Bahadur Chitrakar were both born in 1900, they both graduated from the Calcutta Government School of Art, yet they belonged to different strata of society.

135

Left: This finely executed 17th-century *thangka* depicts the multi-headed and multi-armed Lakshmi Divyashori. It hangs in the National Art Gallery, Bhaktapur, and measures 85 x 118 centimetres.

Right: Although this 18th-century naive painting also uses religious symbolism, it represents a break with the rigid rules of *thangka* art. Entitled *Gorkha Palace*, it shows a brick palace amid mountainous surroundings; in the foreground is a Gurkha regiment, totally out of proportion to the giant Brahma bulls in a neighbouring field. The painting measures 120 x 80 centimetres and hangs in the National Art Gallery in Bhaktapur.

Maskey was a high-caste Newar; Tej Bahadur was a Chitrakar, of the traditional painting class, far down the caste ladder from his colleague. Between them, they radically changed the medieval cultural attitudes of Kathmandu. Maskey opened the doors of the arts to all castes, for he had done the unacceptable: a high caste had entered a low-caste profession. Meanwhile, Tej Bahadur introduced personal expression into the Chitrakar caste. Both painters were naturalists, and although they felt under some obligation to paint flattering portraits of the ruling class who had supported their studies, they were also daring enough to depict social realism. They inspired a new generation of painters to venture out uncompromisingly on their own. Painters who had

formerly served society with unquestioning obedience, now dictated the terms.

Manohar Man Poon is one of this new breed. Although he is of the Chitrakar caste, he is more rebellious than Tej Bahadur — Poon's uncle and oil and watercolour teacher — ever dared to be. There are no sweet portraits in his folio, rather a penetrating, disturbing look at Nepalese society. Like Van Gogh, he has inspired a reputation as a mysterious, unsociable, eccentric who lives in poverty amongst an indifferent populace. Poon was born in 1922. As a youth he was introduced to his family's artistic heritage and to the mysterious art of decorating sacred shrines, a secretive profession known only to a few artisans. When he was seventeen, Poon promised his father, also his drawing master, that he would dedicate his life to painting. Since then, he has never deviated from his task of glorifying and recording Newar social and religious life in his own free style, an odd blend of East and West, but somehow traditionally Nepalese.

Oil paintings by Newar artist Manohar Man Poon (born 1922), show his gift for lending a touch of mystery to scenes of traditional Nepalese life. The portrait (right) is entitled *Nepali Woman*; the group scene (above) is *Nam Sanggati — Praying to the Gods*. Both paintings are in the Lisa Van Gruisen Collection.

Through all these contemporary changes there was a dedicated band of thangka painters who never abandoned their devotional iconographic style, supported by the general population far more than misunderstood moderns are. Out in the distant valleys and hill settlements, the Tamang people fill this gap. Tamang means "horse trader" in Tibetan, and perhaps long ago they practised this trade, but today most of them are farmers, porters and craftsmen. They practise Tibetan Buddhism, their priests are known as *lamas*, and every sizeable village has a monastery and at least one thangka painter, also known as a lama, who meets the people's artistic demands.

Binod Moktan grew up in a village like this in the

mountainous Sindupalchok district of East Nepal. While his Lama father performed *pujas* and attended to the religious needs of the community, Binod spent his time hanging about his uncle's thangka workshop. In 1974, at the age of twelve, he received his formal art instruction and only two years later his skills had become so well known that other village youths started coming to him for tuition. Newar art dealers from Kathmandu often travelled to these remote valleys, to search out new talent and to purchase thangkas for their city galleries, for by this time tourism had reached Nepal and these unique paintings were once again in demand. They recognised Binod's budding talent and inspired by this, and eager for some schooling and electricity, he and his brother moved to Kathmandu, set up an atelier, and began a lucrative business of exporting their Tibetan-style artworks to Europe. Binod could have continued painting

Nepalese thangka painters are now forgoing the Tibetan style and reviving the ancient art of Newar *paubha* painting.

Left: *Namsangati Lakeswar* **by Deepak Joshi (born 1962) depicts an incarnation of Buddha, symbolizing love and sympathy, seated on a pedestal of lotus flowers which floats on the cosmic ocean.**

Right: *Harit Tara — The Green Tara* **by Dinesh Charah Shrestha (born 1965) shows a popular Buddhist goddess who according to tradition was a 7th-century Newar princess who introduced Buddhism to Tibet.**

thangkas for a living, but destiny intervened in the shape of Desmond Doig, a writer, photographer, artist, adventurer and long-time resident of Kathmandu with a keen interest in thangkas. Doig bought a Kalachakra *mandala* from Binod and noticed how the artist used special landscape effects in the background. He suggested that Binod try watercolour landscape painting using these same stylised mountains and petrified clouds. It was a casual suggestion, but for an iconographic painter one that demanded a totally new way of looking at art. Binod was trained to paint for worship; landscape was merely a backdrop for the deity, or a filler in the mandala. Yet he took up the challenge and produced his first landscape. It was of Bodhnath Stupa, where the all-seeing eyes peer down

Landscape painting, once used solely for *thangka* backgrounds, has become an art form on its own. These naive watercolours are the work of Nepal's foremost landscape painter, Binod Moktan (born 1962). The vertical painting (left) is of Thyangboche monastery, high in the Khumbu Himal; the horizontal painting (above) is of Swayambhunath Temple.

across a colourful naive setting while devotees spun prayer wheels. As a backdrop were mystical stylised peaks and those swirling primitive clouds of his thangka paintings. There was no looking back. Doig bought his first work and then organised an exhibition at Kathmandu's October Gallery. Eighteen of 23 works sold in the first day. Binod now works exclusively in his own unique landscape style, but he still runs the thangka atelier with his brother, for it helps him keep in touch with his roots.

These days, galleries, workshops and ateliers abound in Kathmandu, and junk work turned out for money-conscious tourists floods the market. But among these are traditional thangka and paubha painters who have not succumbed wholly to commercialism, who still grind their own colours and produce astonishing works of art. These traditionalists, the uncompromising contemporaries like Poon and the naive landscapes of Binod maintain Kathmandu's reputation as the cultural heart of the Himalayas.

Of Cycles and Seasons

Before the Industrial Revolution, which sounded a death knell for the traditional farming communities of Europe, everyone's life swayed to seasonal rhythms. As on the 15th-century French calendar I studied in my schoolgirl art history classes. Pictured for each month was a map of the heavens: above were the celestial cycles and below scenes of the terrestrial activities prescribed for that particular month. March showed a farmer urging on his oxen as he ploughed his fields; July pictured women reaping. There were the fallow winter months when men went hunting, and the joyous festivities of the harvest month. In the background of all these scenes were walled medieval towns and castles.

Although its fortified walls have long gone, the Kathmandu Valley retains the feudal feeling of that old French calendar. The Nepalese still live by the old saying that for everything there is a season. Their ancient lunar calendar continues to determine the annual cycle of seasons and festivals herald each changing phase. On these auspicious occasions, the gods are propitiated to bring favourable results during the upcoming cycle.

Despite the urban sprawl of Kathmandu and the few fledgling industries, the valley is predominantly agricultural, and farming methods differ little from those depicted on the medieval French calendar, almost all crops cultivated by hand. The seasonal procession is illustrated by the valley's changing colours. Come early spring, the fields are yellow with mustard blossoms, then the first rice seedlings bring a pale green hue. A vivid carpet of sub-tropical growth blankets the land during the monsoon. Then, during the October harvest season, the entire valley turns a burnished gold.

Tilling the soil since remote times, the Newars have

Late afternoon sunlight streams through trees that line the road to Bhaktapur, silhouetting a farmer who trudges home with a basket of fertilizer on his back. The harvest is over and the fields must be prepared for yet another cycle of the farming season.

145

developed an agriculture that is far superior to the rest of Nepal. They carefully built their crowded towns and cities on the hills and ridges to preserve as much of the precious alluvial flat land as possible. Land means rice, and rice means life, and many of the most popular annual festivals are those that are inextricably bound with the rice cycle.

In April or May, according to the astrologer's calculations, after the chariot procession of the rain-giving Red Machhendrenath, there is usually a downpour sufficient to water the fields. A few weeks later, on the occasion of the Warrior God Kumar's birthday, known as Sithinakha, rice seeds are planted and corn is sown in the hills, for this marks the beginning of the rainy season. On this day, the farmers

The Newars not only adorned the valley with their rich culture and arts, but evolved one of the most intricate agricultural systems in the world. They terraced the valley to make the most of its rich alluvial soil, which they cultivate today using the same hand implements as their ancestors.

leave their beloved musical instruments in the care of Nasa Deo, the god of music, for there will be no time to play them until the planting is complete, and for three months no major festival interrupts their work until the Ghanta Karna, the night of the devil — the traditional rice planting finale day. It is believed that on this night evil spirits roam the land, just as the destructive demon Ghanta Karna once did until a frog tricked him and he fell into a well and was drowned. Frogs are still honoured by special rituals, but they are not the only animals that have their own day in Kathmandu's crowded festival agenda, for cows, dogs and even crows have their own traditional events when they are given special food and blessings and treated as kings for a day.

After the rice planting is over the festival calendar really hots up, for there is leisure time aplenty while the monsoon rains do the farmer's work. There is Gunla,

Buddha's sacred month; Naga Panchhami, the Snake God's Day; and Janai Purnima, when the Brahmin's sacred body threads are renewed. On the day after this, known as Gai Jatra, each family who has experienced a death in the year past, honours their deceased by dressing a boy as a highly decorated cow. The child then participates in a procession along with musicians and the family priests. Cows are the helpers who smooth the way to heaven, and back in the Malla times, when real cows were used in Gai Jatra, this was the way the ruler kept a census of his people. By counting the cows, he knew how many subjects had died that year.

More festivals follow in rapid succession. There's Krishna's Birthday, Nepalese Father's Day and the Teej

Brata, a time when women fast and bathe at Pashupatinath to ensure a happy and productive marriage for the year ahead. In September, the spectacular Indrajatra, an eight-day festival, honours Lord Indra, the Ruler of Heaven and his goddess mother, who farmers believe supply the valley with its vital fog and dew (known as "milk") for ripening their harvest during the dry autumn months. A towering pole representing Indra is erected at Kathmandu's Hanuman Dhoka palace, huge fierce masks of Bhairav are put on display, traditional dances are staged, and the Kumari, the living virgin goddess, is pulled through the city's streets in her ponderous chariot.

But Dasain, in the midst of the autumn harvest, is by far the longest and most auspicious festival of the year. It is a joyous time that commemorates the Ramayana time when the all-powerful goddess Durga triumphed over evil. Innumerable *pujas* are enacted, processions and pageants are held, families are united and thousands of animals are

Above: Seen from the lofty vantage point of Nagarkot, over 2,000 metres high, the Manohara River twists like a silvery ribbon across the floor of the Kathmandu Valley.

Right: In a village still swathed in morning mist, a youth flings himself skywards on a bamboo swing specially constructed for the Dasain festival.

Above: These hard-working women, like walking haystacks, carry ricestalks on their backs along the old route that links Changu Narayan with Bhaktapur. Corn is grown in the summer and when dried packed into conical stooks beside each rural home.

Right: Woven mats covered with shiny red chillies, a spicy staple of Nepalese cuisine, dry in the sun. Everyone is preparing for the winter season, for the cold winds are already sweeping down from the snow-capped Himalayas.

150

sacrificed. The markets in every town and city — especially Asan Tole in Kathmandu — are jammed with shoppers, for at Dasain everyone buys new clothes and the other ingredients needed for the festivities.

In the countryside there is action of a different kind, for the rice harvest is in full swing. Along the old Bhaktapur road, in a large field of terraced golden rice, two dozen men and women with small crescent-shaped knives harvest their paddy. They converge on the ricefield like the beaters in a tiger hunt. Men wearing long flapping shirts and jaunty caps, gather armloads of the freshly-cut grain and ferry it across the hand-made paths that serve as walls for each terrace. In a nearby stubble field, they join other labourers who are feeding the rice into a foot-powered threshing machine. Its *choonk, choonk* noise echoes across the fields, where other harvests are taking place. Across the valley floor, women in turquoise and red shirts bob up and down like ships in a sea of golden rice. A farmer's wife tosses back her waist-length braid of hair and balancing a brass water jug on her hips, she weaves through the fields bringing refreshment to the thirsty harvesters. In the villages, every available flat sunny place is covered in mats of drying unhusked rice. Women using long poles with a wooden half circle on the ends rake the grain about, exposing it to the sun. In front of a house with pumpkins on its roof, an area of ground is being cleared and

painted with a fresh mixture of cow dung and clay in readiness for the harvest. The sounds of laughing harvesters drift across the fields. This is Dasain, the most joyous time of the year in the valley.

Along every road to Kathmandu, herds of sheep and goats are holding up the traffic. They are obviously part of yesterday's newspaper article in *The Rising Nepal.* "Nepal Food Corporation this year is bringing in 6,000 mountain sheep and goats from the Tibet Autonomous Region of the People's Republic of China and 4,000 goats from the Terai region for the Dasain festival." The ones I see are coming from the Tibetan side, long-haired mountain goats that seem oblivious to the bloody fate that awaits them. For tomorrow is the great sacrificial ninth day of the festival, the day of Syako Tyako, when it is said "the more you kill, the more you gain." Goddess Durga prefers the blood of uncastrated black male buffaloes, but in the old days humans were sometimes sacrificed to bring even more benefits for the year ahead. Indeed, it is whispered, that this ancient custom is still secretly performed on this eve, the dark night of Dasain. Writing in 1819, Francis Hamilton, in *An Account of the*

Kingdom of Nepal, and of the Territories Annexed to This Dominion by House of Gurkha, mentions that every twelve years the Gurkha king offers a solemn sacrifice, when among those slayed are two men of a rank worthy to carry the sacred thread (Brahmins). "They are made drunk, they are carried to the sanctuary, their necks are sliced and the spray of blood is directed on the idols, then with their skulls, cups are made to be used in these horrible rites." But, as Hamilton remarks, buffaloes, rams, cocks and ducks were the usual prey.

The following day I watch as animals meet their fate. In the Kot Courtyard, scores of animals are sacrificed and their blood smeared on the army's banners and standards to ensure a victorious year ahead. In the streets of Bhaktapur,

October heralds the annual rice harvest in the Kathmandu Valley. Under bright-blue autumn skies, throughout the terraced fields, workers are reaping the golden grain. Women winnow in the traditional fashion by tossing the rice in the air to separate chaff from grain. In each town square and over every flat sunny space, unhusked rice is spread to dry.

I look on as a newly-sacrificed buffalo is covered in straw and set alight. When the hair is singed off, the buffalo is butchered and distributed around the neighbourhood, for all will eat meat tonight. I am also an onlooker to bus and car blessings, wherein goats are sacrificed and their blood sprayed over wheels and bumpers and even sprinkled over screwdrivers, wrenches and jacks artfully arranged on a hessian bag in front of the car. Goat's hair adorns the grilles and steering wheels. The smell of blood, sweat and animal fear hangs heavy in the air. A man holding his baby runs up to me and joyously exclaims, "today all the demons are killed and now the gods are happy." But it is all a little overwhelming for me and I yearn for the fresh, unbloodied spaces of the countryside. I decide to walk to Nagarkot, situated on the rim of hills that encircles the Kathmandu Valley, where I drink of the mountains in all their pristine purity. Blood sacrifices are an intrical part of the festivities, but it's hard for me to relate to it as a joyous occasion. Then I spy, on the outskirts of town,

Right: A garlanded Nepalese officiates at the annual military sacrifices in the old armoury or *kot*, across the square from the Hanuman Dhoka, as a women looks on (below). On this day, animals are slaughtered by the hundreds to honour Durga, the goddess of victory and might.

a scene that for me is more reminiscent of happy festive times, for there in a field under a makeshift big top, is a circus. I pay my three rupees and join the merry crowd of urchins and town boys who sit on tiered planks, watching two young female contortionists perform acrobatics on a tiny table balanced on bottles filled with pink liquid. It is a circus run by children for children, as the only adult participant is a listless old man who plays the background percussion with a battered side drum and cymbals. Even the ringmaster is just a youth. The rapt crowd watches while a black-and-white speckled goat walks across a metal tightrope, pirouetting

when its youthful sequin-shirted trainer taps its hoofs with a rattan cane. When the goat nearly falls off its perch, the urchins laugh out loud, but nothing moved them quite as much as the young clown who apes the other performers, tells dirty jokes, and always lands on his backside after futile acrobatic manoevures. The boys hang on his every word, tears of joy streaming down their cheeks, especially when he reluctantly plays the victim for the knife-thrower and manages to duck the whirling blades. There is juggling, more acrobatics, and then a girl contortionist is hoisted to a rather ricketty trapeze where she swings back and forth for the grand finale of the children's circus. I walk down the hill and out along the road to Nagarkot with the urchins, laughter still ringing in my ears. It is a joyous Dasain after all.

I recall that twenty years ago when I first visited Nagarkot, the view was just as it is on this wonderous occasion. The old white-washed lodge I had stayed in is still here, atop of the ridge and surrounded by conifers. It was here, under the spell of the scenery and in the daze of youth, that I had first beheld this marvellous vista — the Vale of Kathmandu on one side and a mountain-filled horizon on the other. I watch until the sun slips over the hills into India, taking the light with it. The valley grows shadowed and dark. I turn around and there are the Himalaya, glowing with the soft pink and magenta of sunset. And under their gaze, the valley folk will go to sleep contented tonight, for another cycle is complete, another successful harvest is over, the demons are exterminated, and the gods in those lofty, glowing realms are appeased. Peace and happiness once more rules over the Kathmandu Valley.

155

After the hard work of rice harvesting is over for another year, the inhabitants of Bhaktapur are entertained by a travelling circus. The townsfolk, lured by the colourful hoardings outside the tent, flock to see contortionists, acrobats, trapeze artists, knife-throwers, jugglers and a spotted goat who walks the tightrope.

157